THE AMAZING ALPHABET

Written, Illustrated, and Designed by
Abigail C. Johnson

Testimony Publishers, LLC.®
Casper, Wyoming

Copyright ©2023. Abigail C. Johnson. All Rights Reserved.

ISBN: 978-1-7360187-7-4 (eBook or Digital)
978-1-736-0187-8-1 (Paperback)
Library of Congress Control Number: 2024906850

No part of this publication may be reproduced, distributed, or transmitted in any form or by any means, including photocopying, recording, or other electronic or mechanical methods, without the prior written permission of the publisher, except in the case of brief quotations embodied in critical reviews and certain other noncommercial uses permitted by copyright law. For permission requests, write to the publisher, addressed "Attention: Permissions Department," at the address below:

Testimony Publishers, LLC.®
300 N. Center Street, Unit 6
Casper, Wyoming 82601
admin@testimonypublishersllc.com
https://www.abigailcjohnson.com

Edited By: Sam Wright, Penguin Random House, USA
Cover Design By: Manuel Quintana, JBook Designs, Abigail C. Johnson, and Testimony Publishers, LLC.®

Dedication

To My Brothers and Sisters –
You inspire me to love and encourage me to be great.
Thank you for being my inspiration for this book.

Love you forever,
Abigail

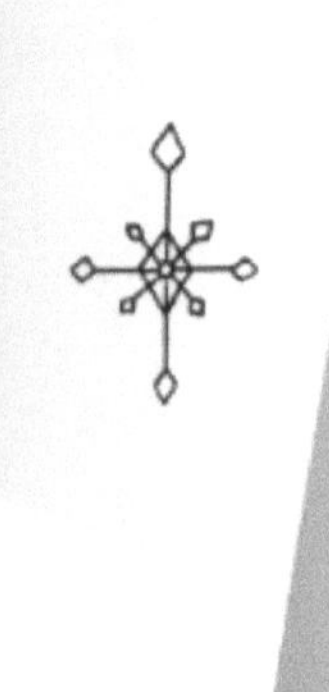

Aa is for Arctic Fox

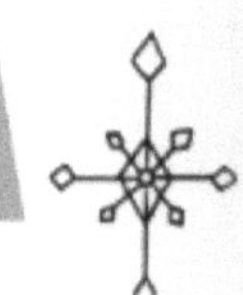

In snow, it's white, in trees, it's brown,
God made its fur to match the ground.

How do you think the Arctic Fox feels in the snow?

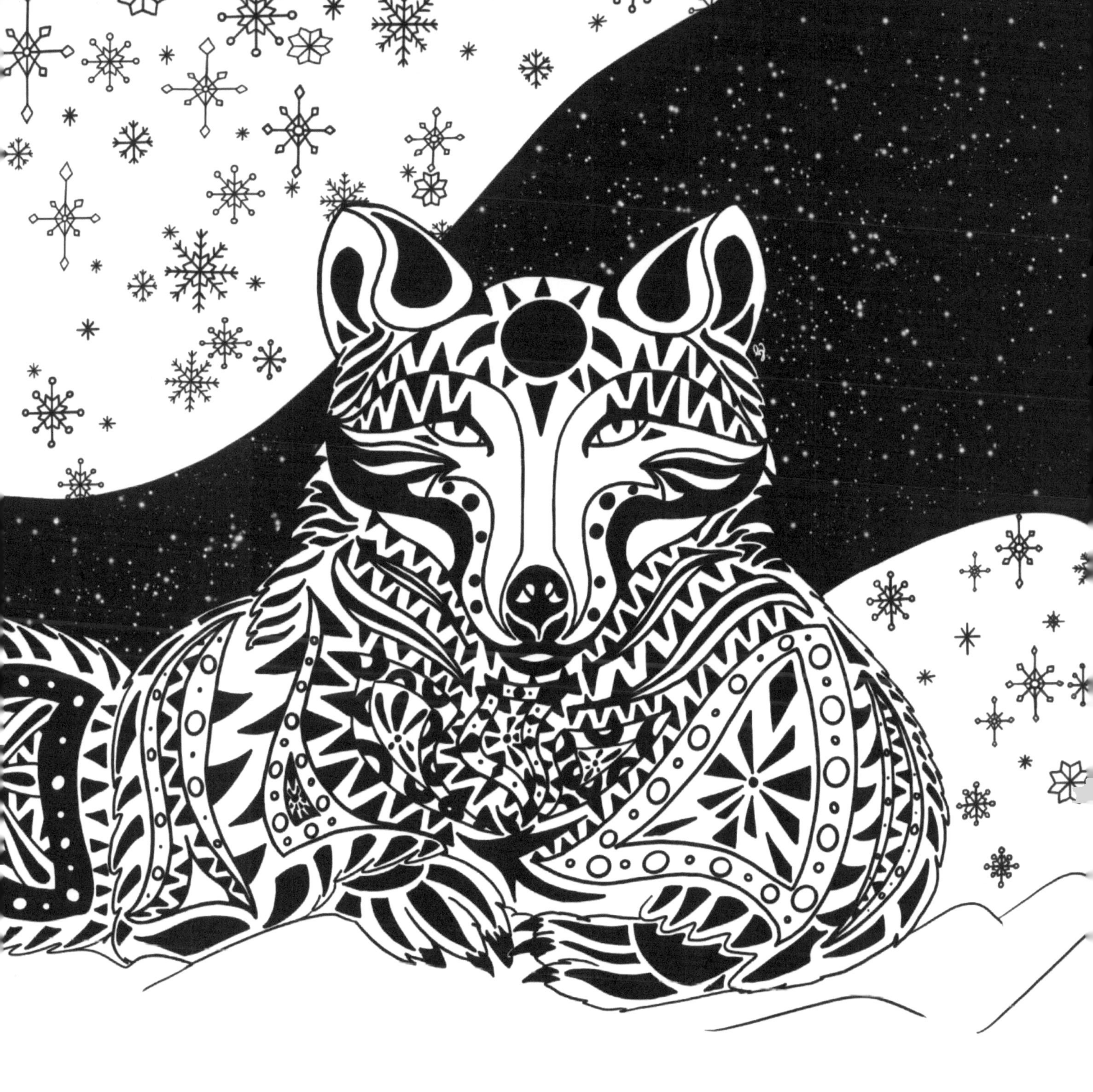

Bb is for Bald Eagle

A bird of prey, regal and bold,
God made its beak, bright as gold.

Can you spread your arms like a Bald Eagle's wings?

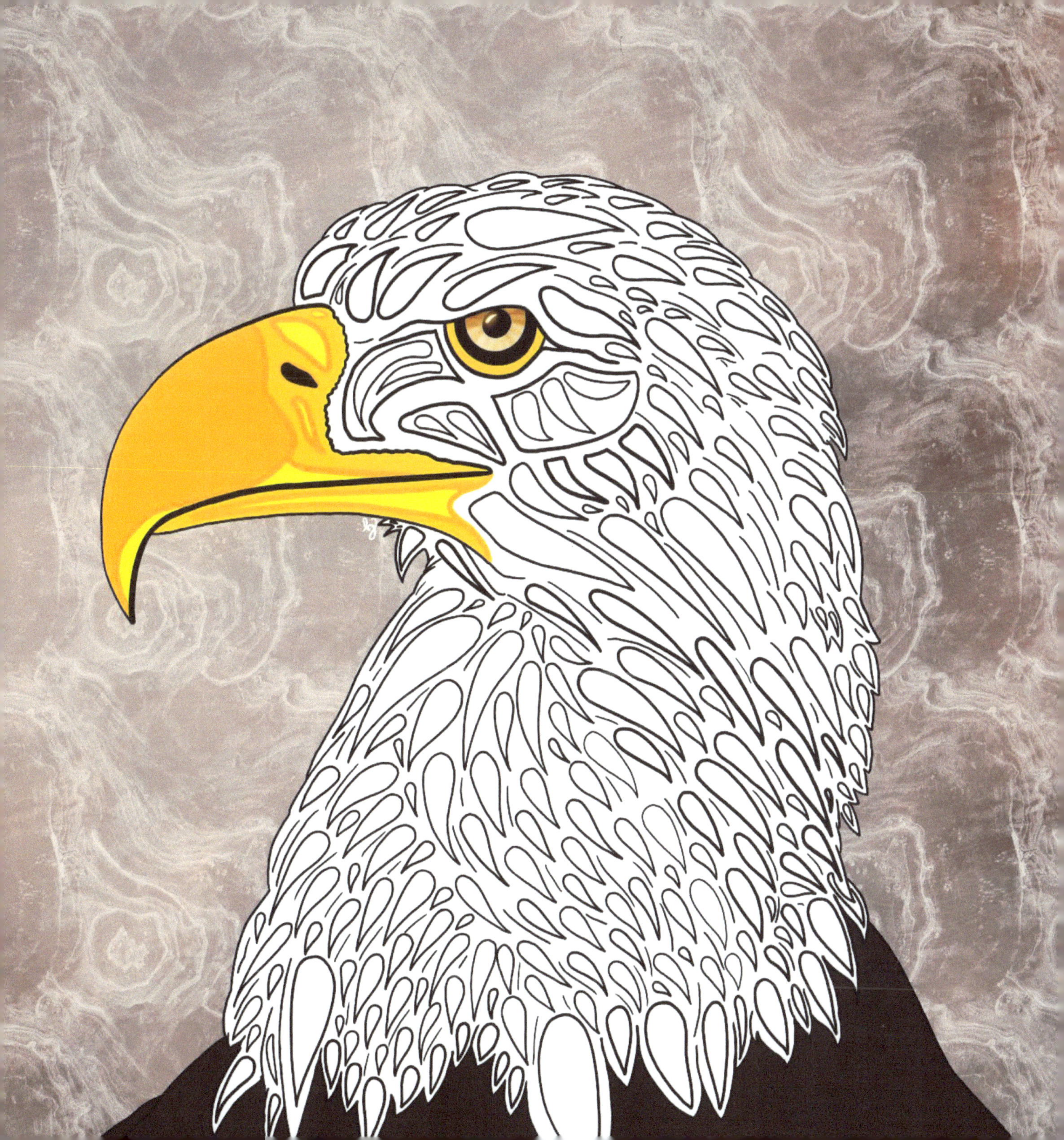

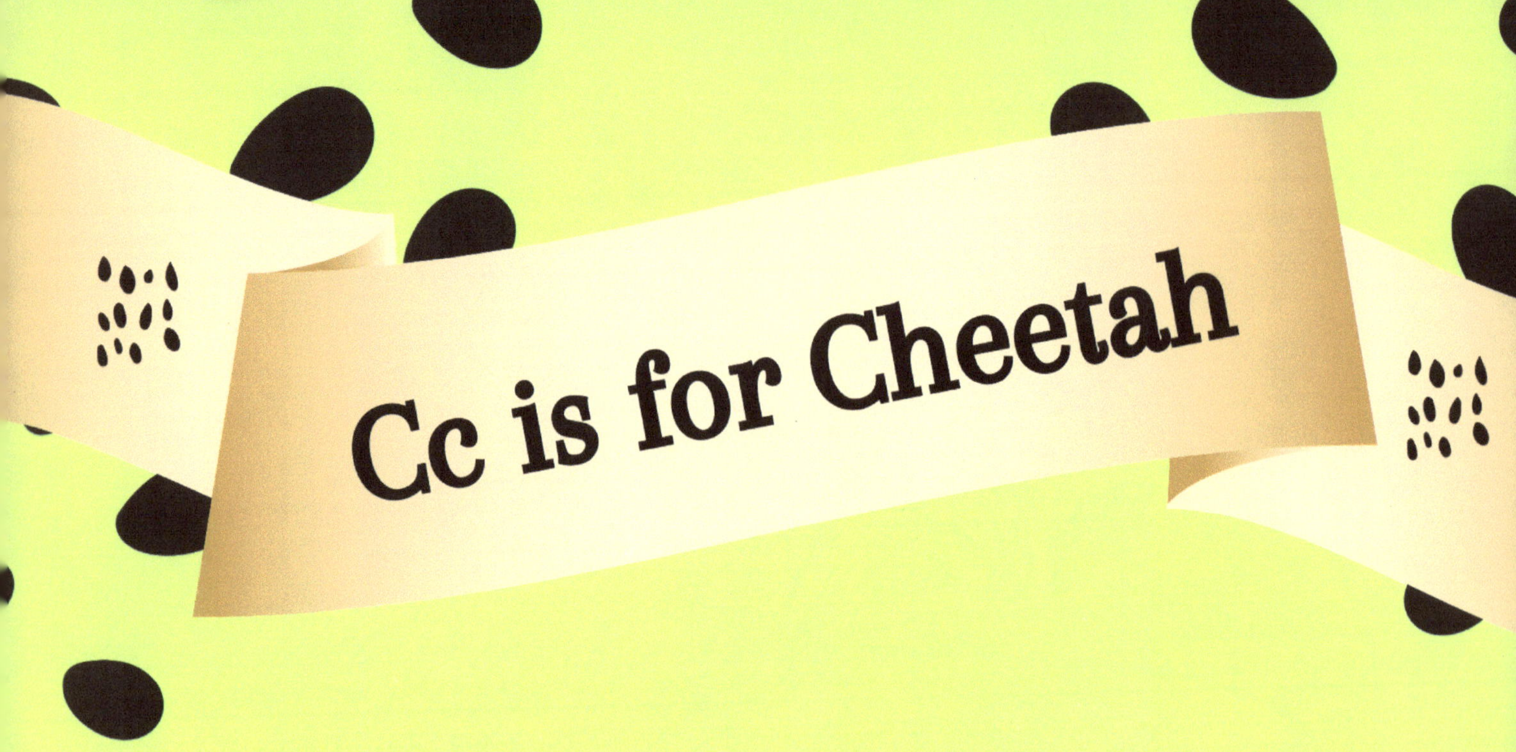

Cc is for Cheetah

Fastest on land, a sight to see,
God made this cat zoom, as quick as can be.

How fast do you think you can run compared to a cheetah?

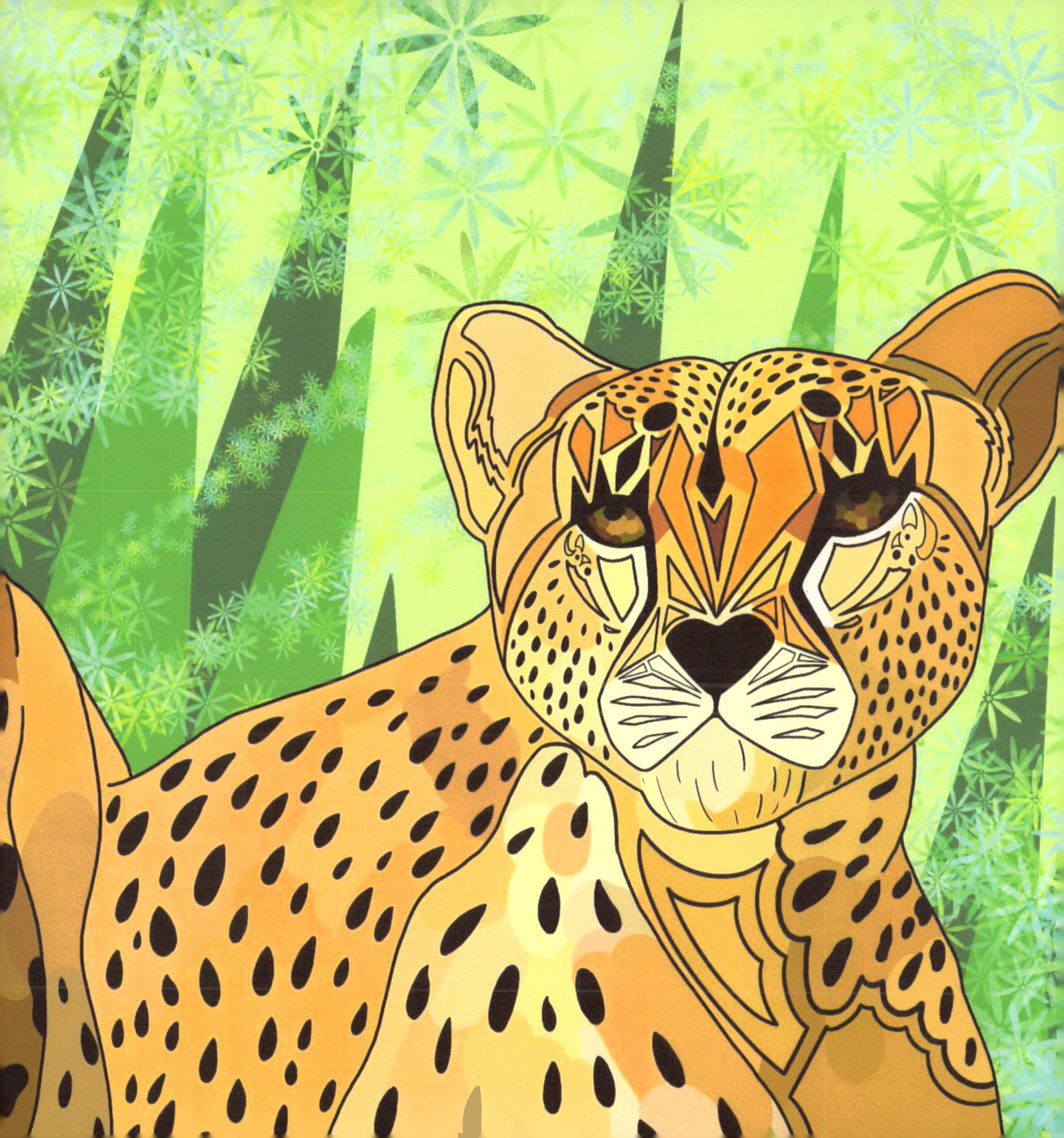

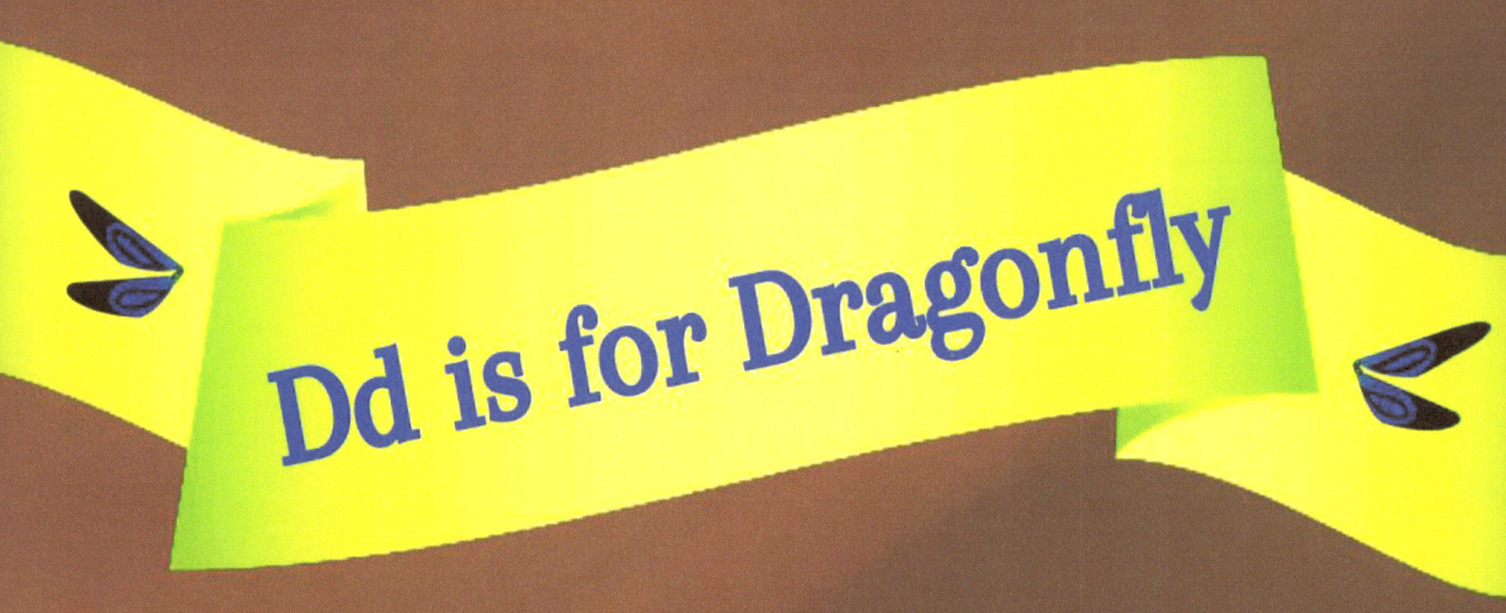

Forwards and Backwards, it flies round-and-round,
God made this insect fly upside down.

Can you spot a dragonfly next time you're outside?

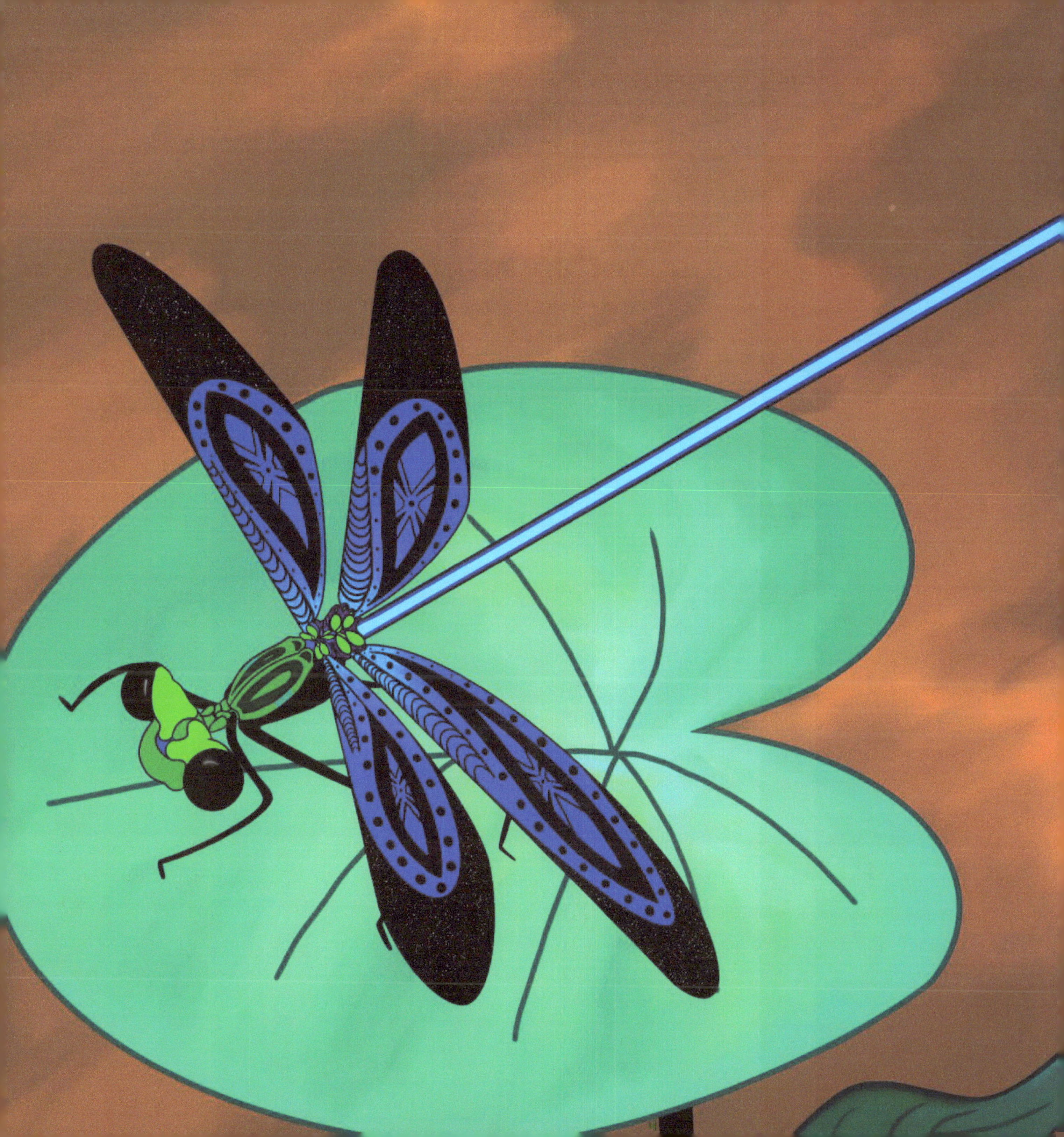

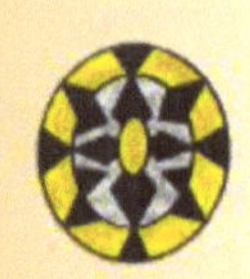

Ee is for Elephant

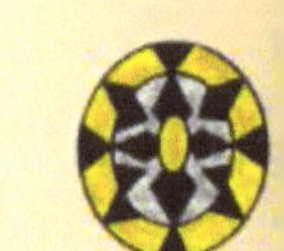

One long trunk, two large ears,
God made this giant tower above its peers.

Have you ever seen an elephant use its trunk?

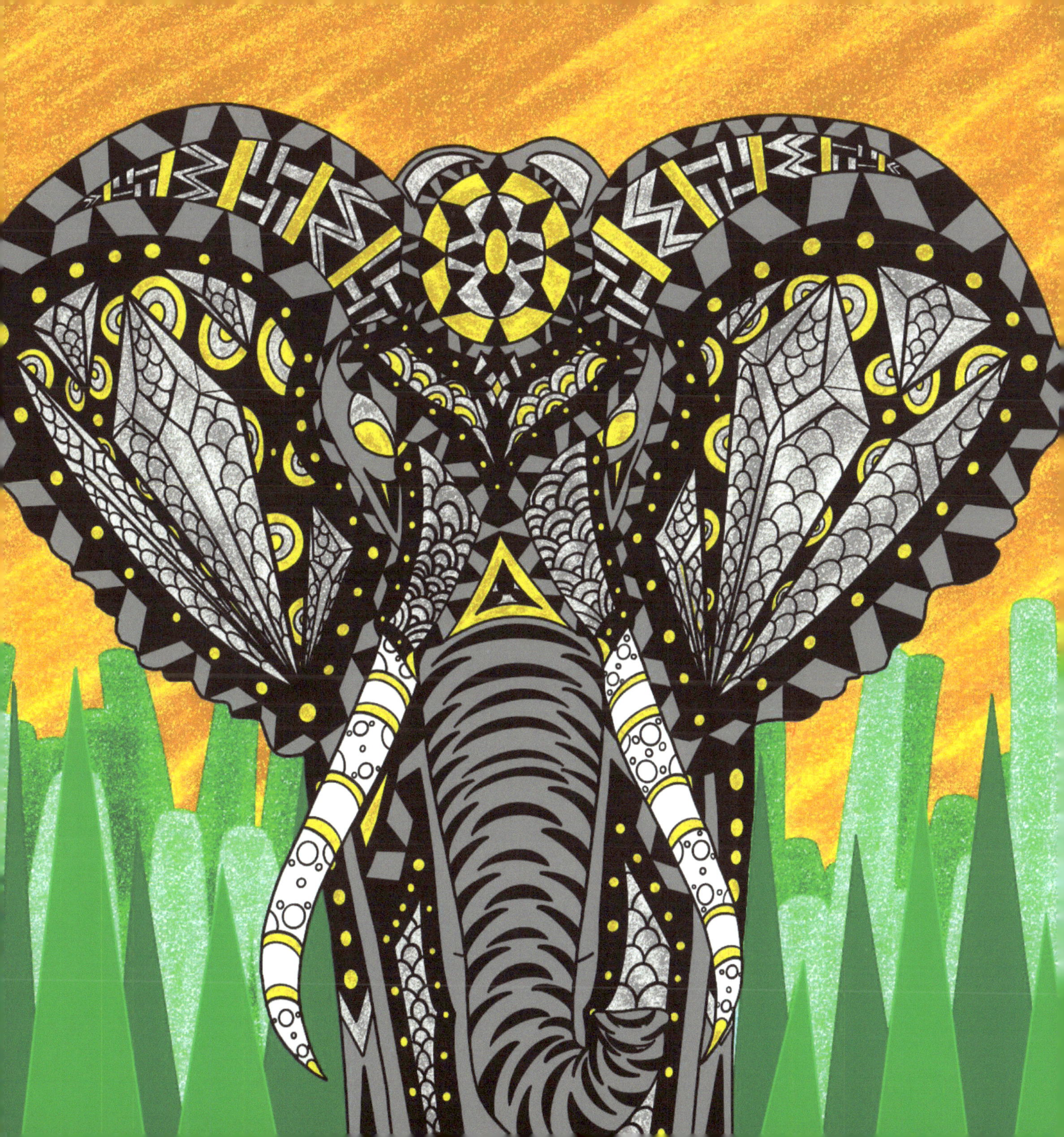

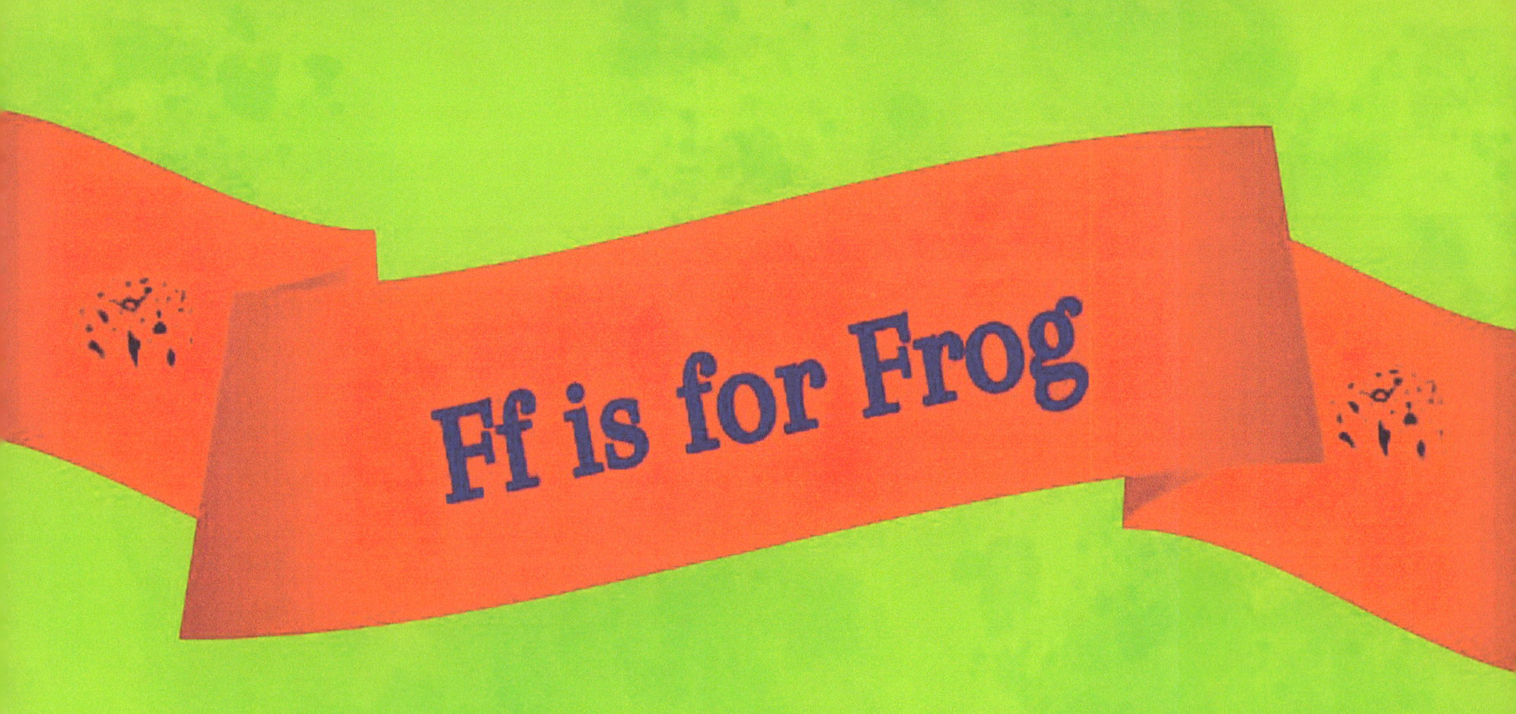

From tiny to big, they leap and they call,
God made the Poison Dart Frog the deadliest of all.

Can you hop like a frog?

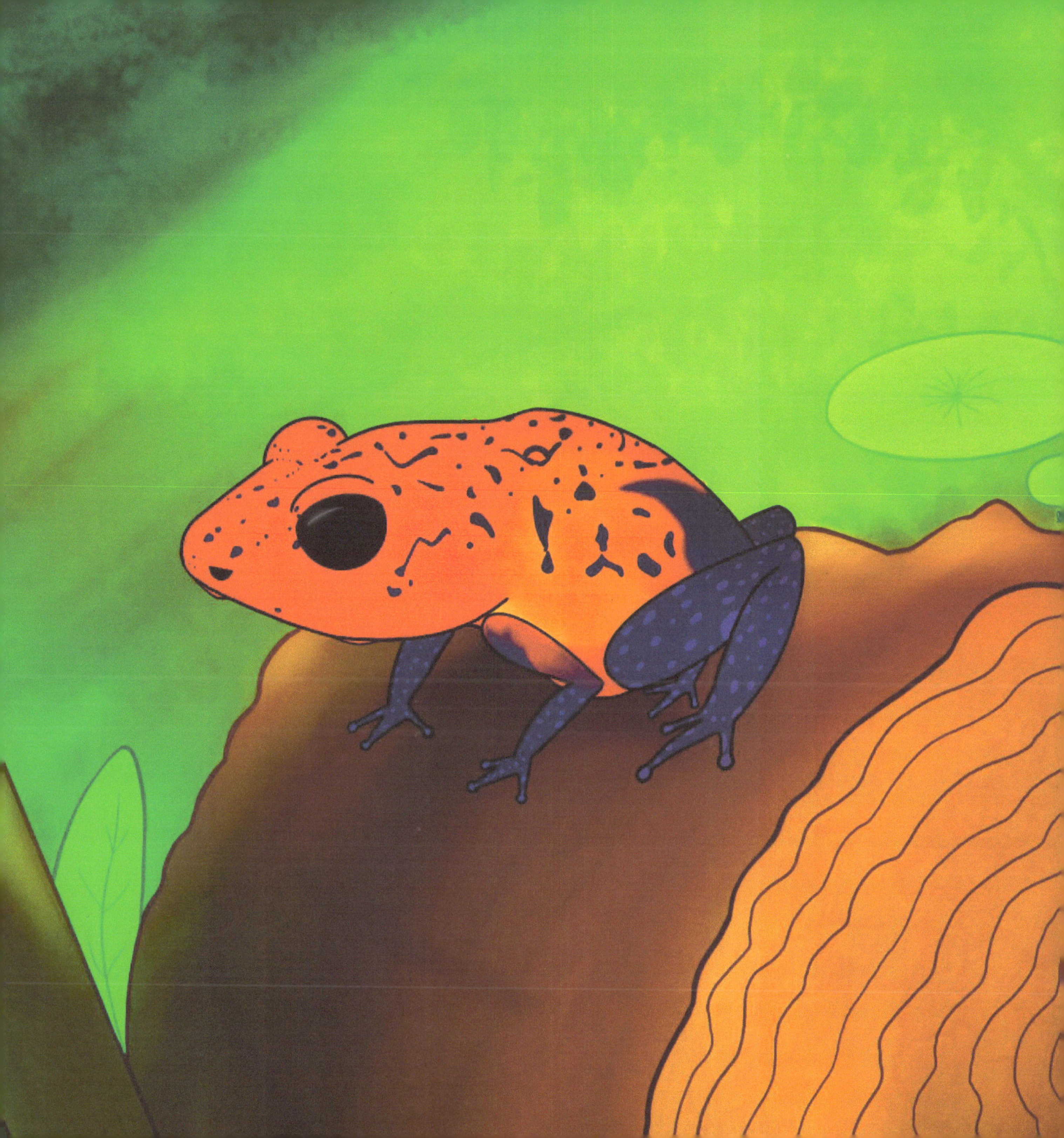

Gg is for Gazelle

Slim and so swift, they march and prance,
God made them love to leap and dance.

Have you ever seen a gazelle prance?

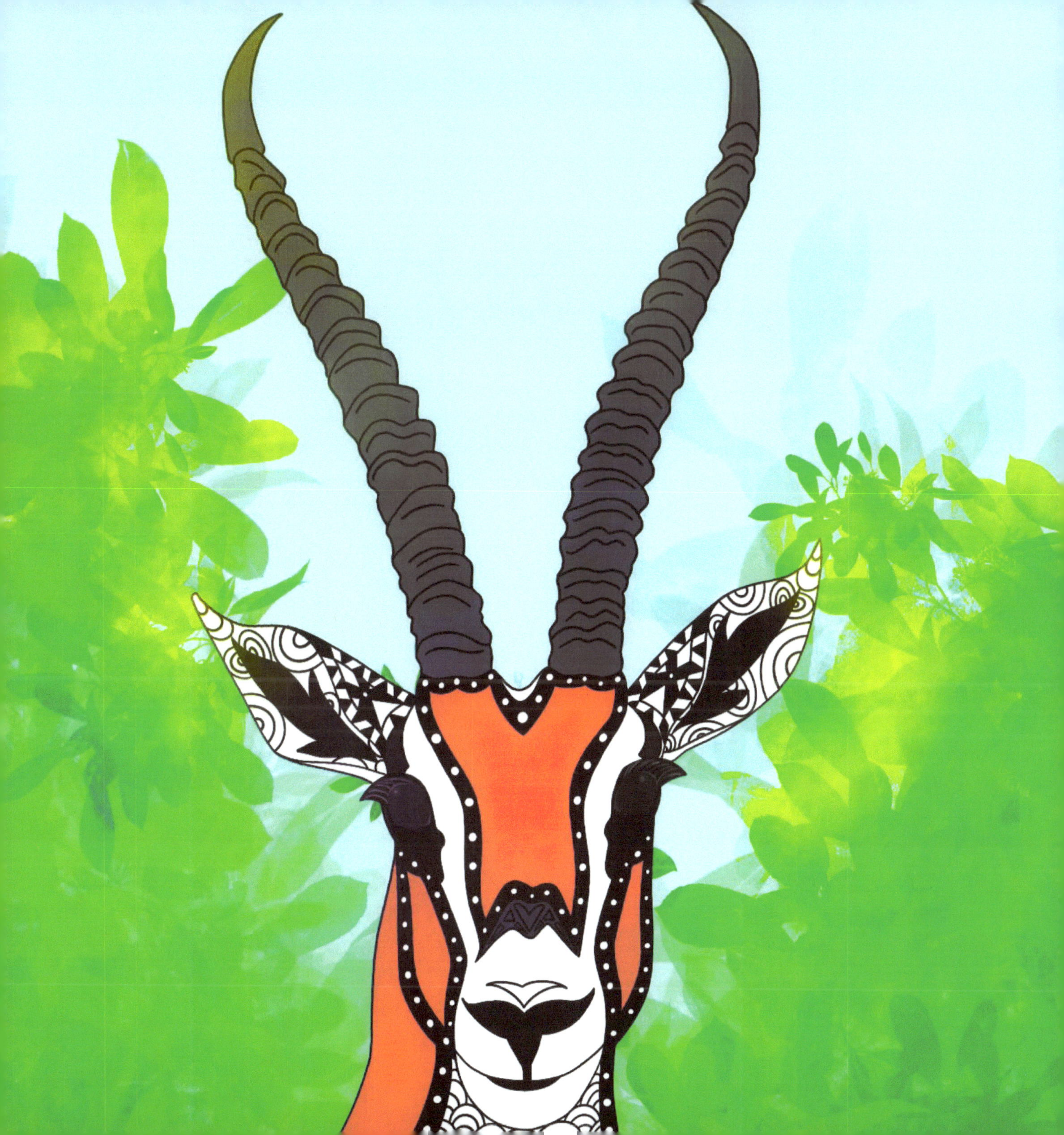

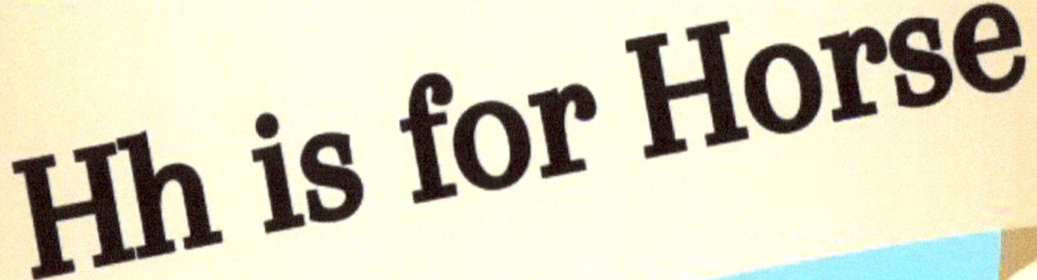

Hh is for Horse

Friesian horses, so black and grand,
God made them trot across the land.

Can you trot like a horse?

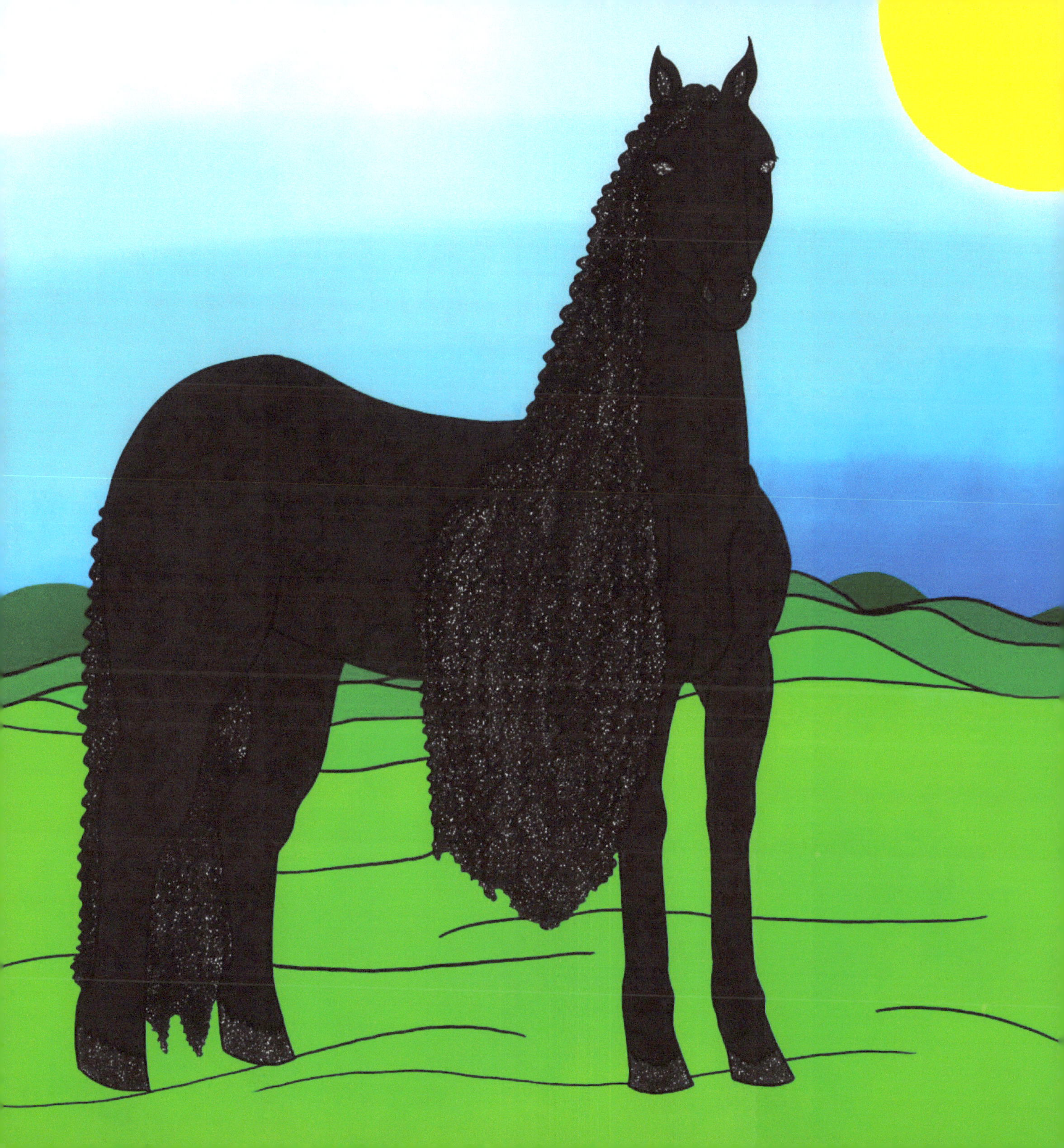

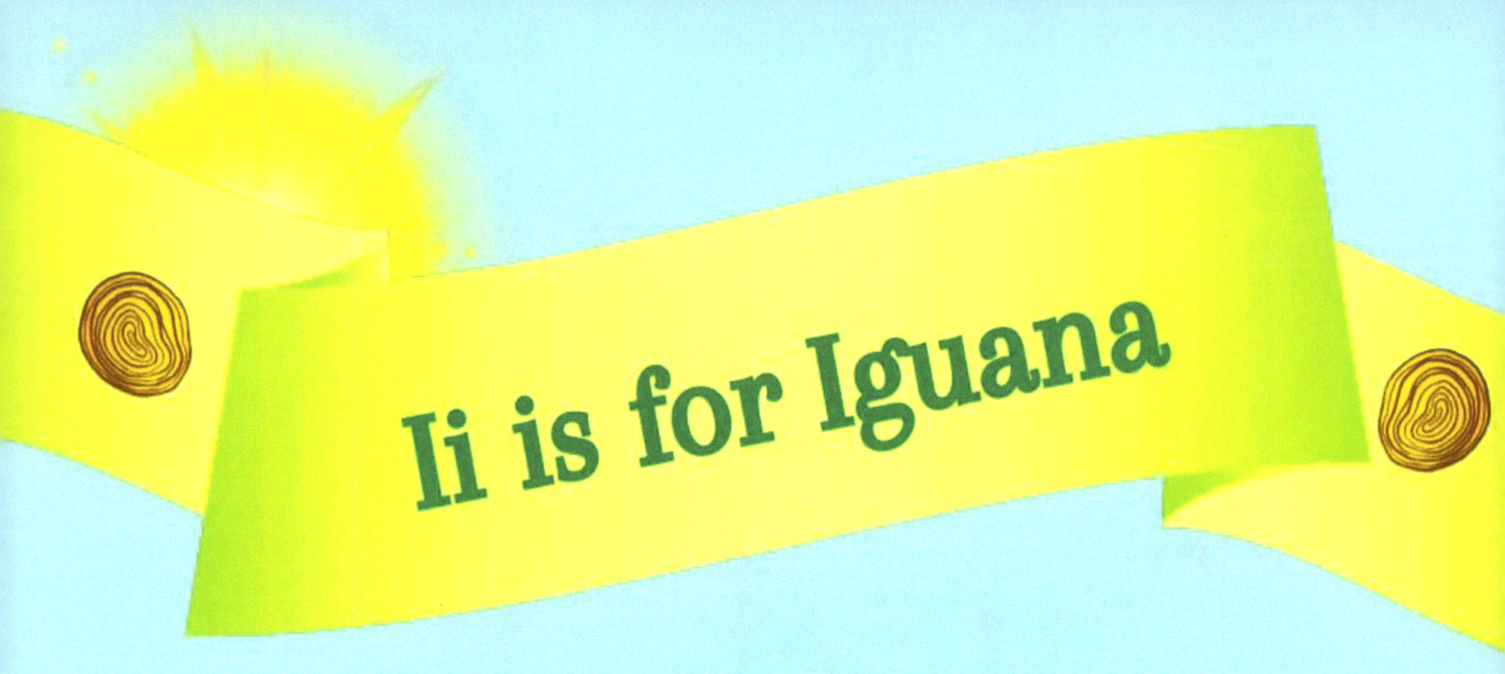

Ii is for Iguana

Loves the sunshine, its tail regrows,
God made it blend in, so its prey never knows.

Would you like to blend in with your surroundings like an iguana?

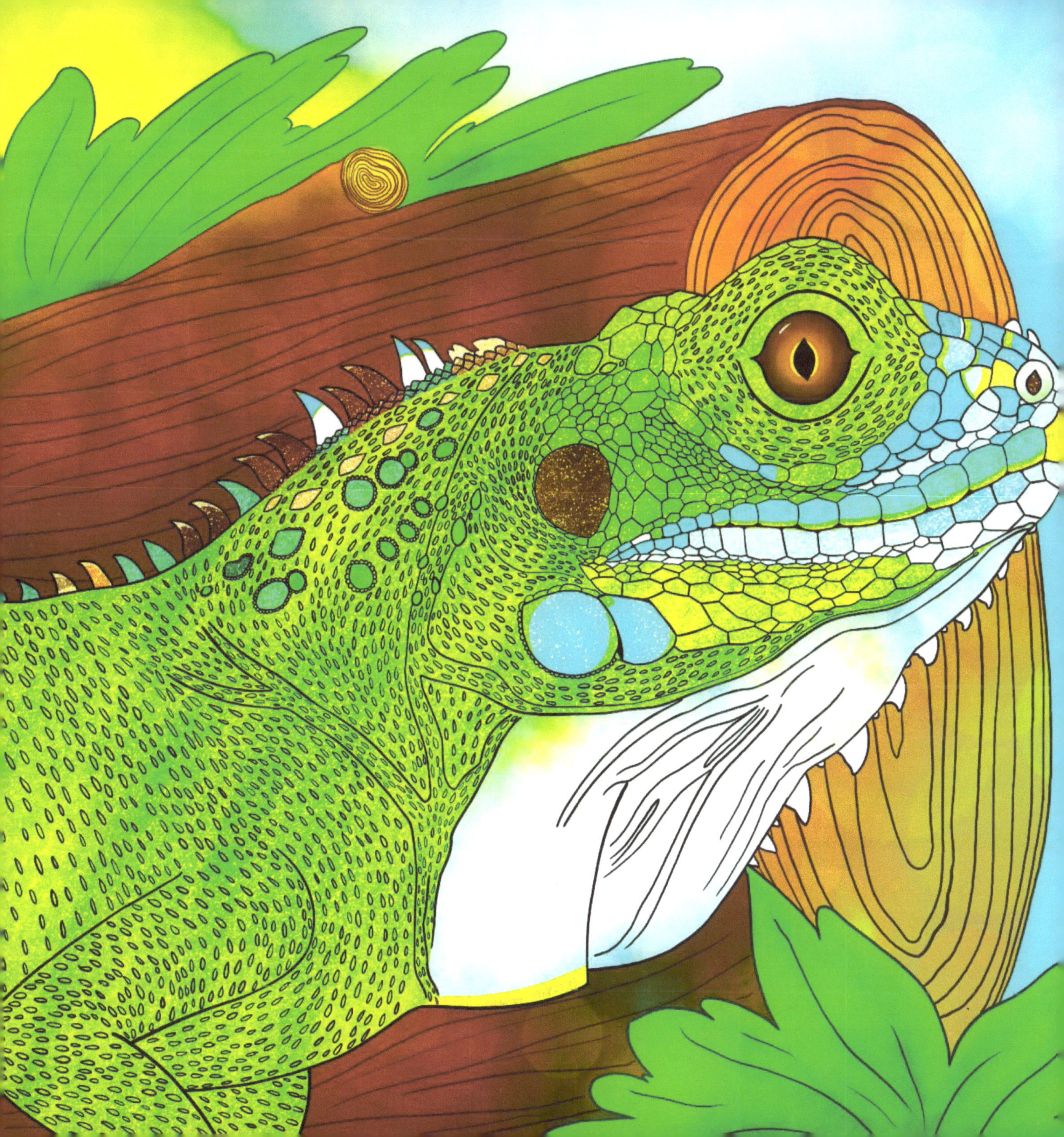

Jj is for Jellyfish

Floats by day, glows by night,
God made its tentacles sting with might.

Have you ever seen a jellyfish in the ocean?

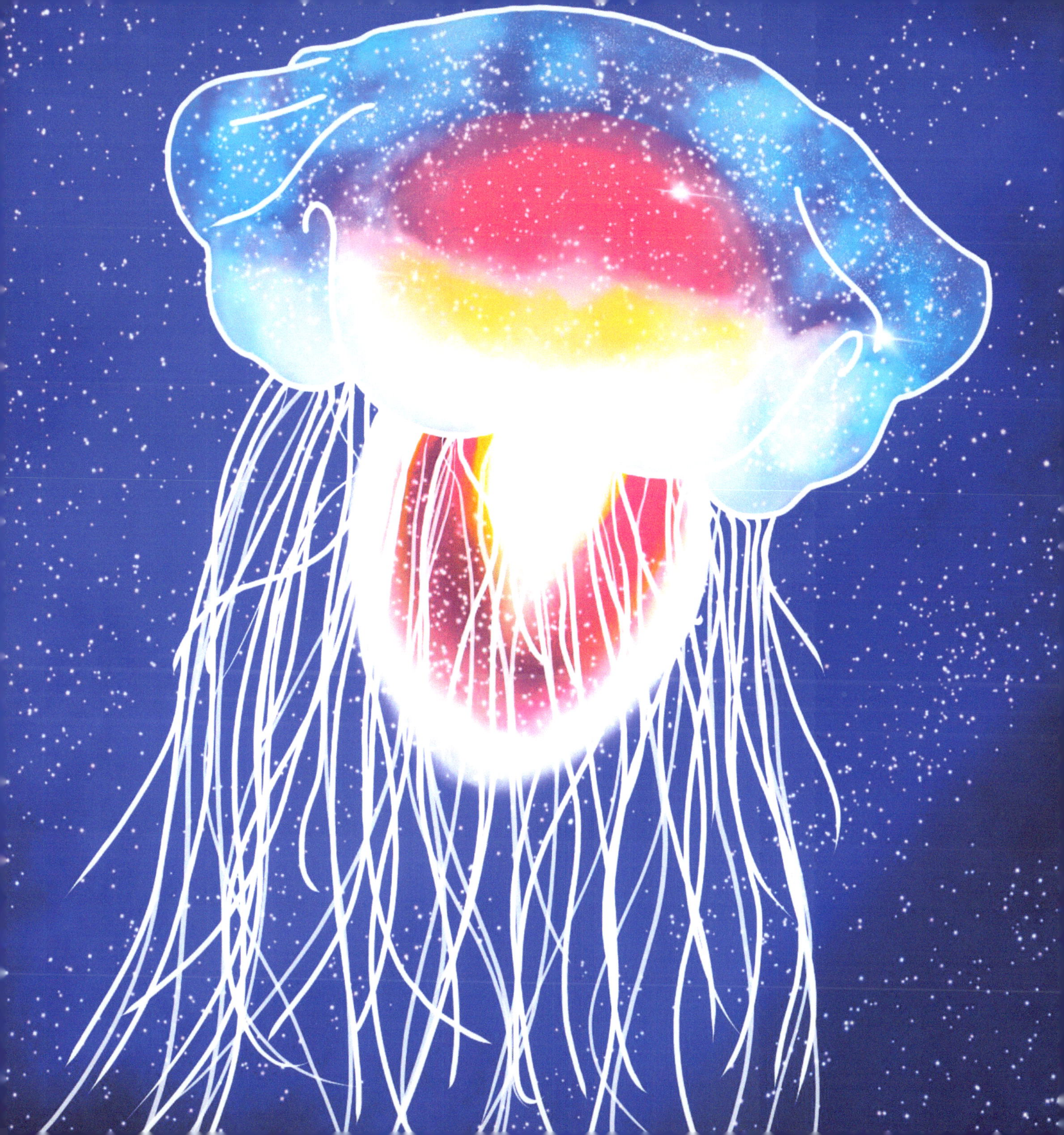

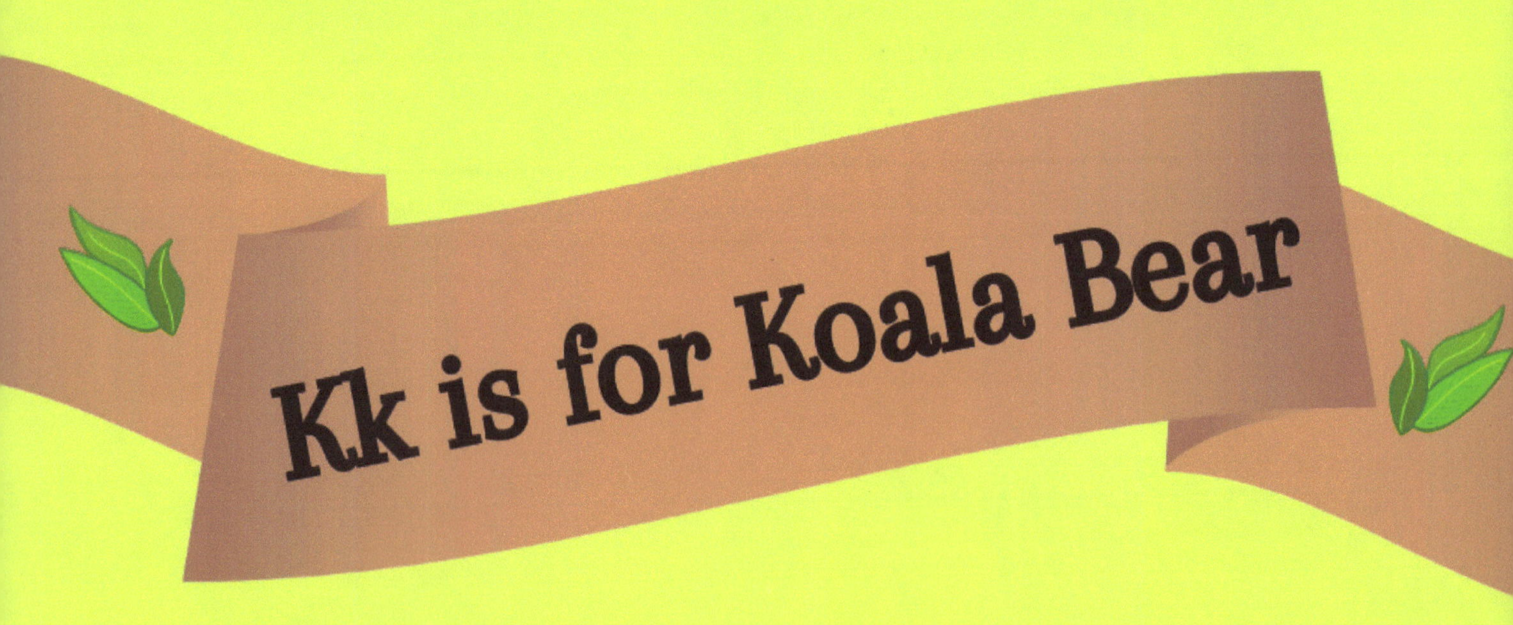

Sleepy, fluffy, it climbs tall trees,
God made this marsupial love eucalyptus leaves.

Can you pretend to munch on leaves
like a koala bear?

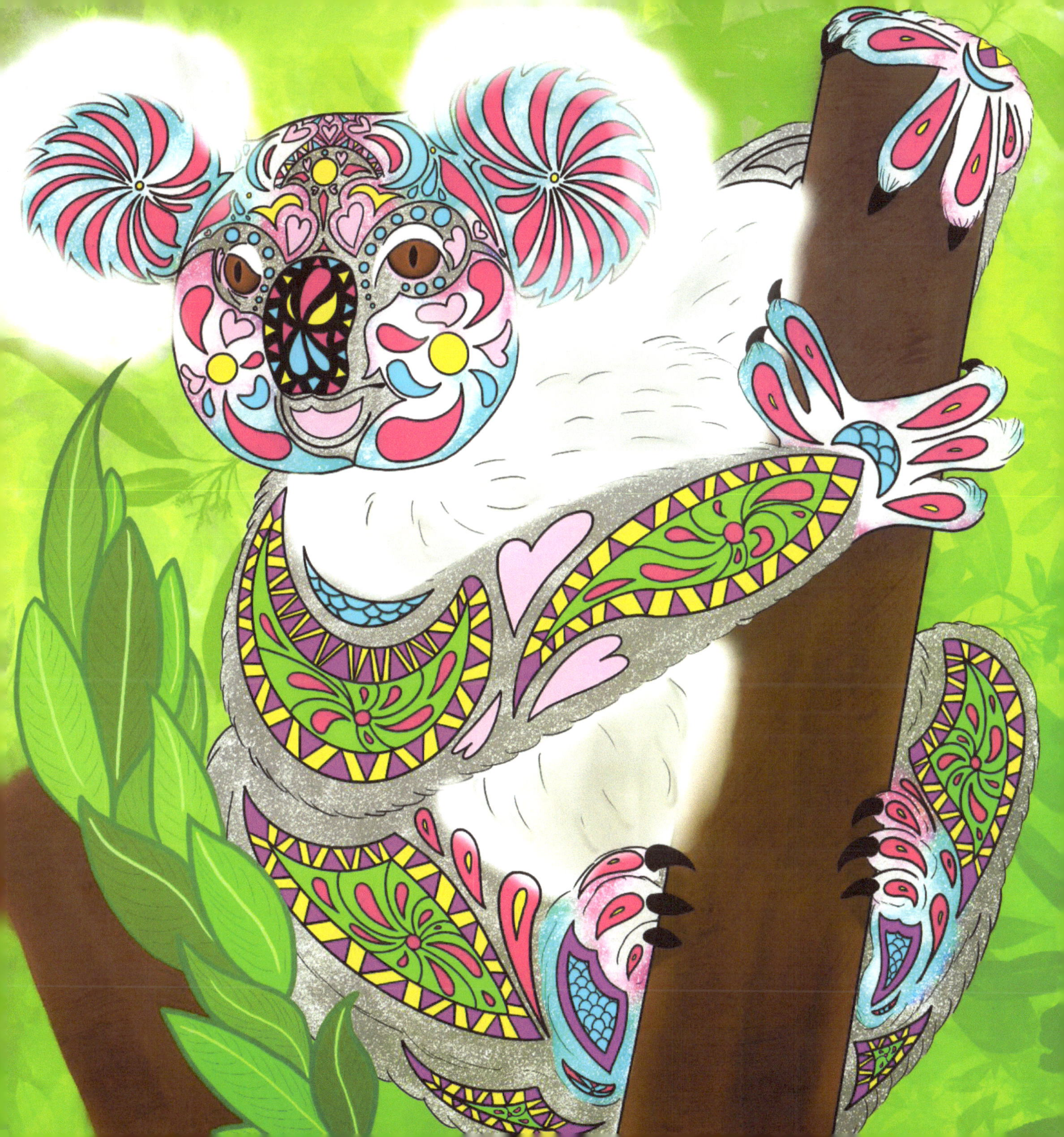

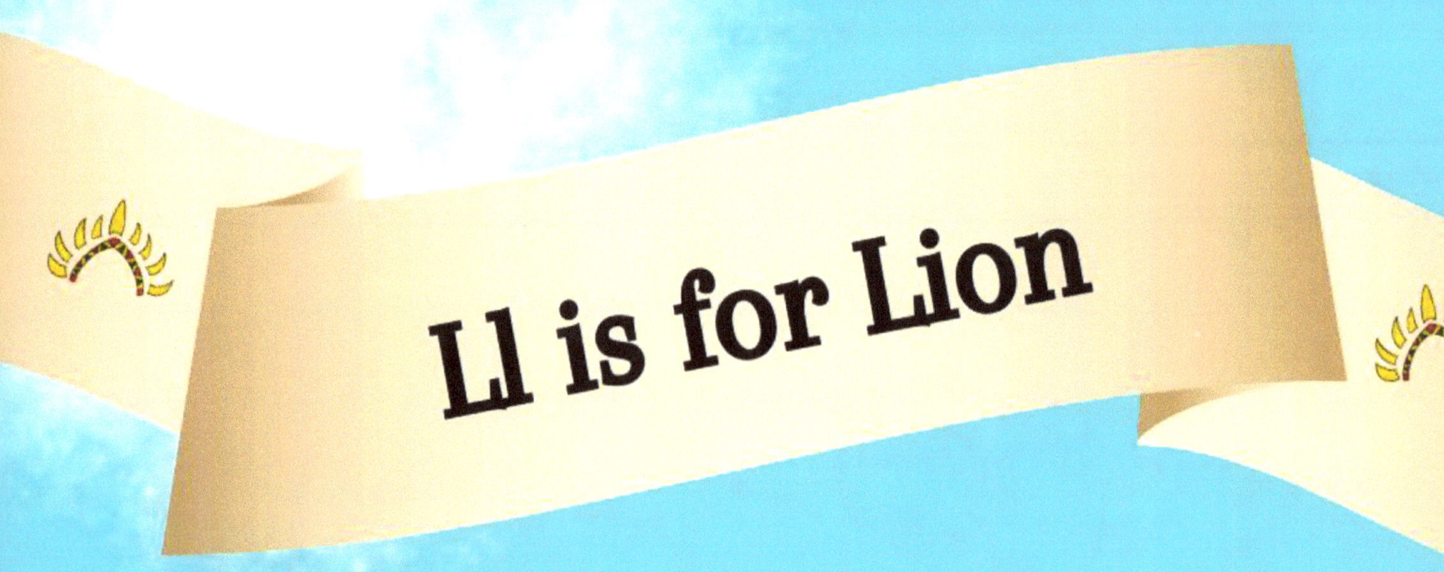

Ll is for Lion

"King of the Jungle," with a roar so loud,
God made this wild cat walk so proud.

Can you roar like a lion?

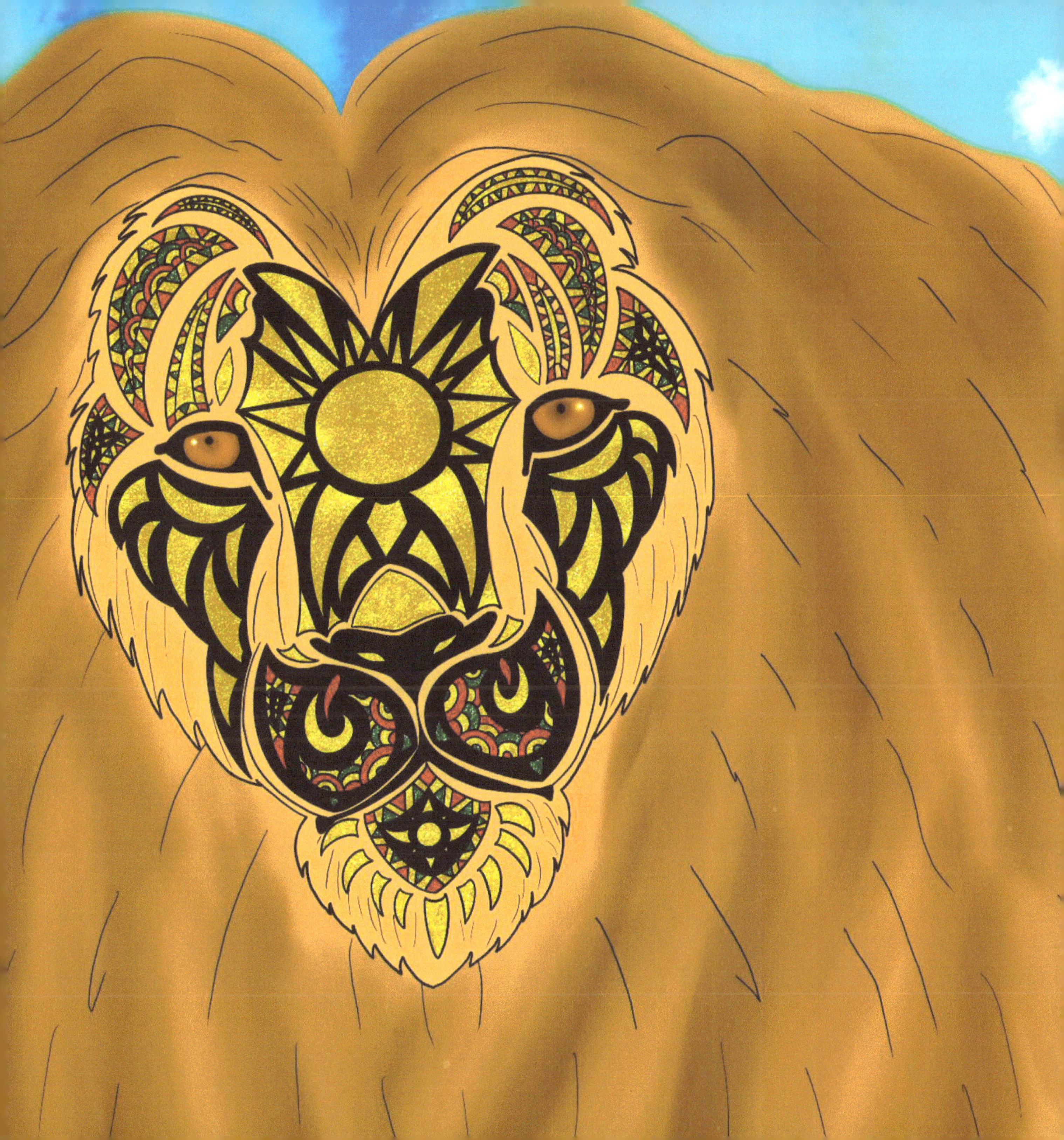

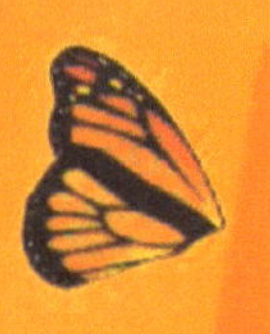

Mm is for Monarch Butterfly

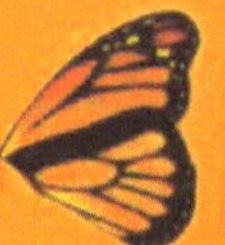

It flutters and flies, round-and-round and back,
God made this insect orange and black.

How far do you think you could fly as a butterfly?

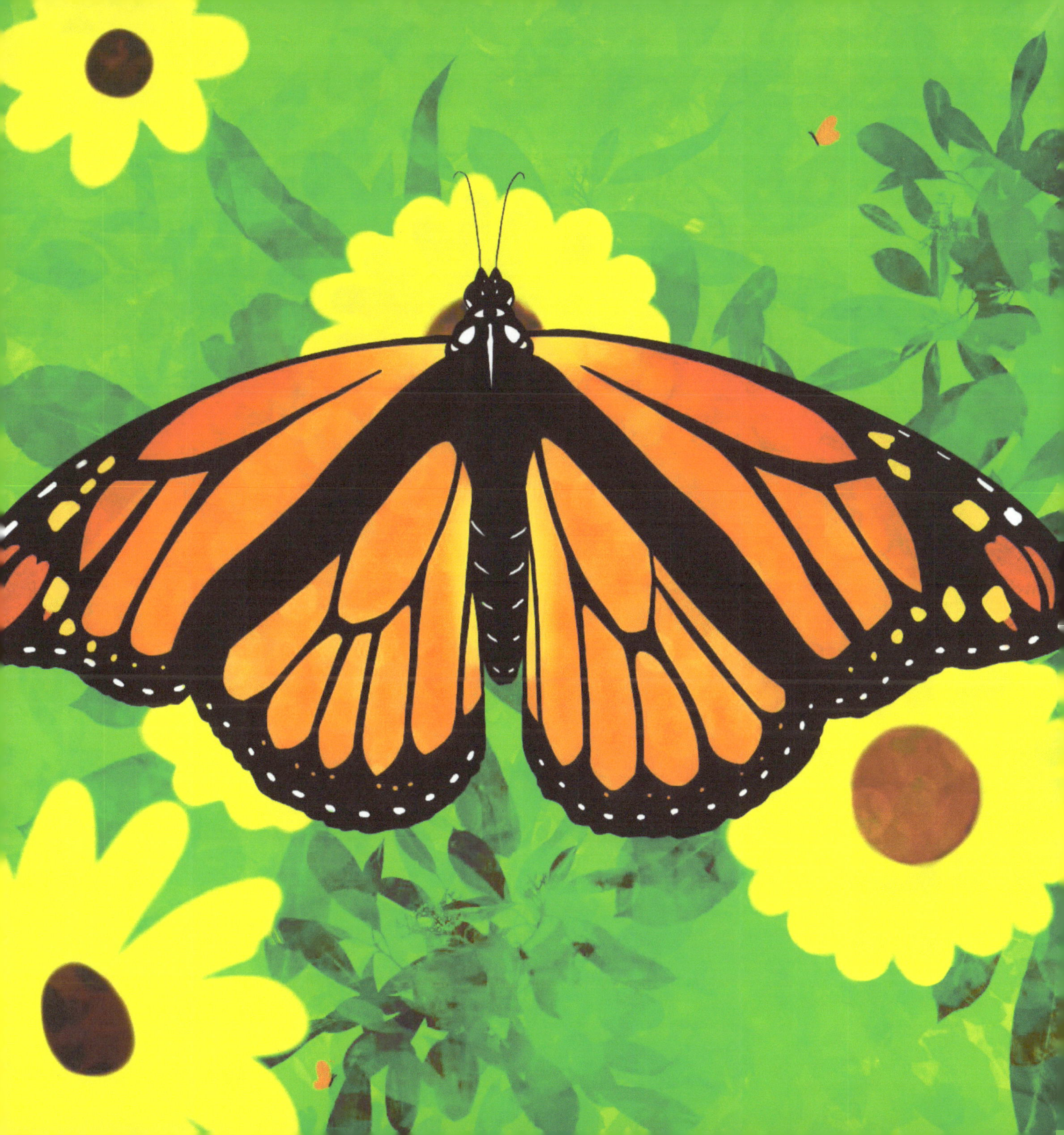

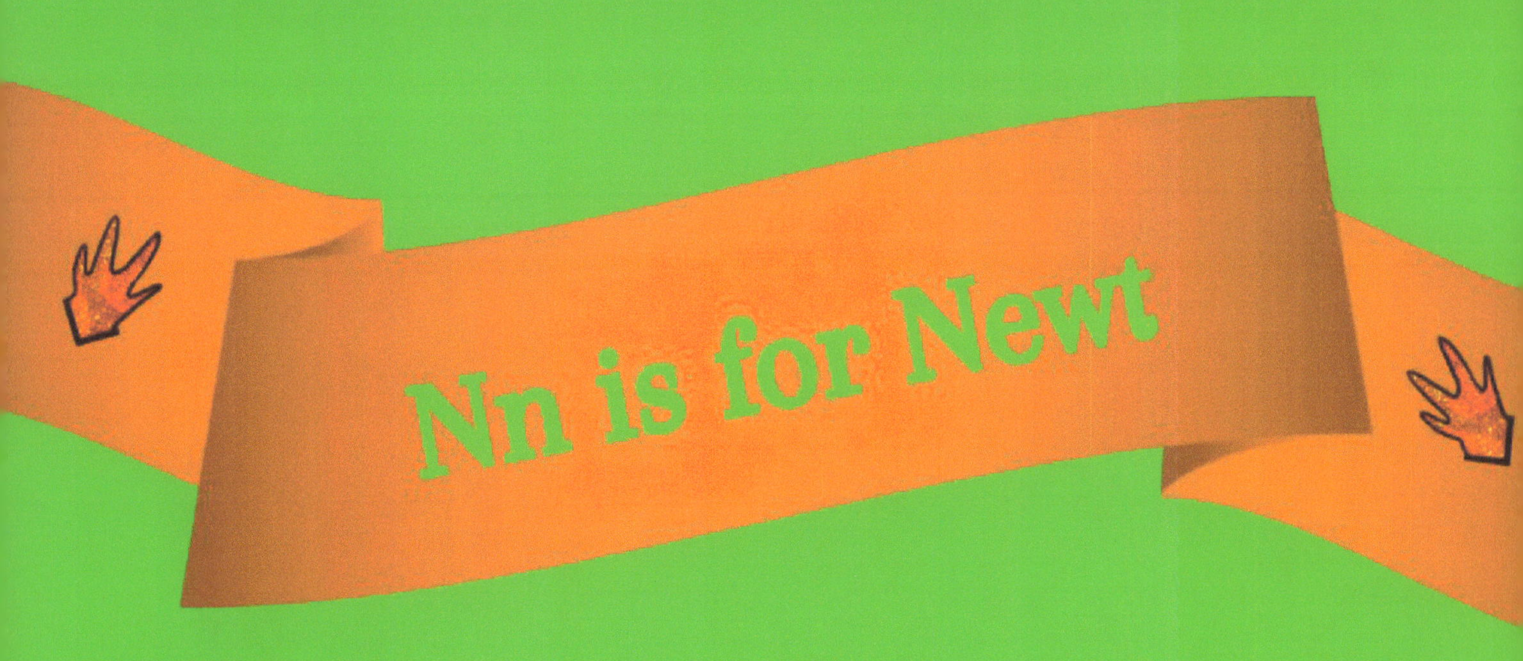

Breathing underwater, and regrowing its hand,
God made this salamander for the sea and land.

Have you ever seen a newt regrow its body parts?

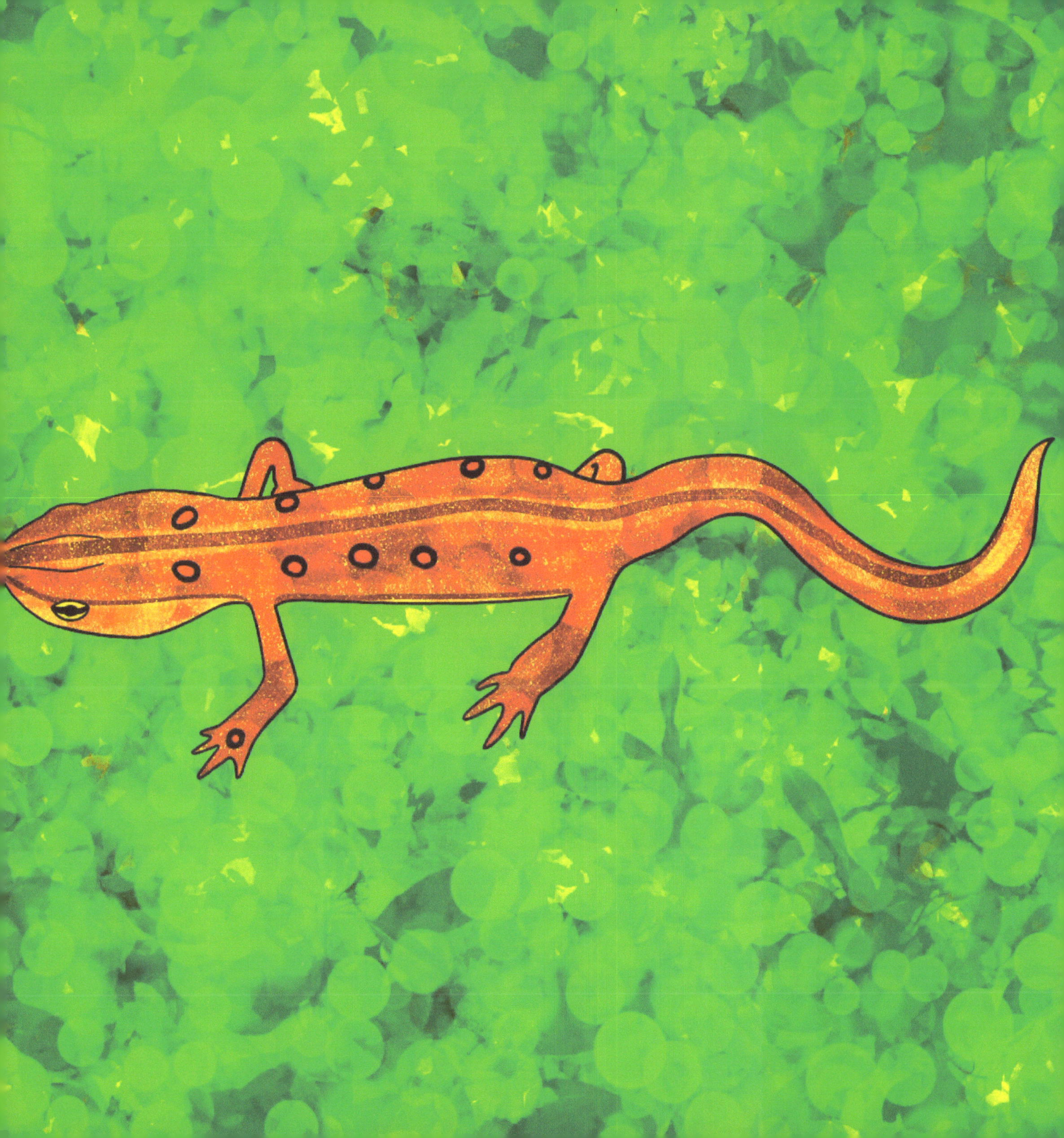

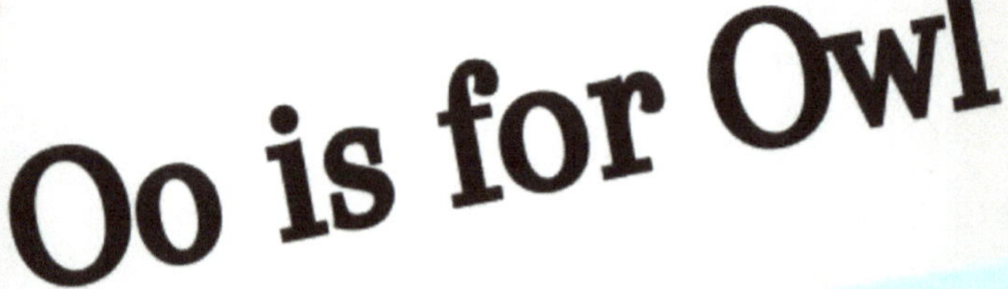

Oo is for Owl

With perfect sight, it hunts at night,
God made this bird silent during flight.

Have you ever seen an owl at night?

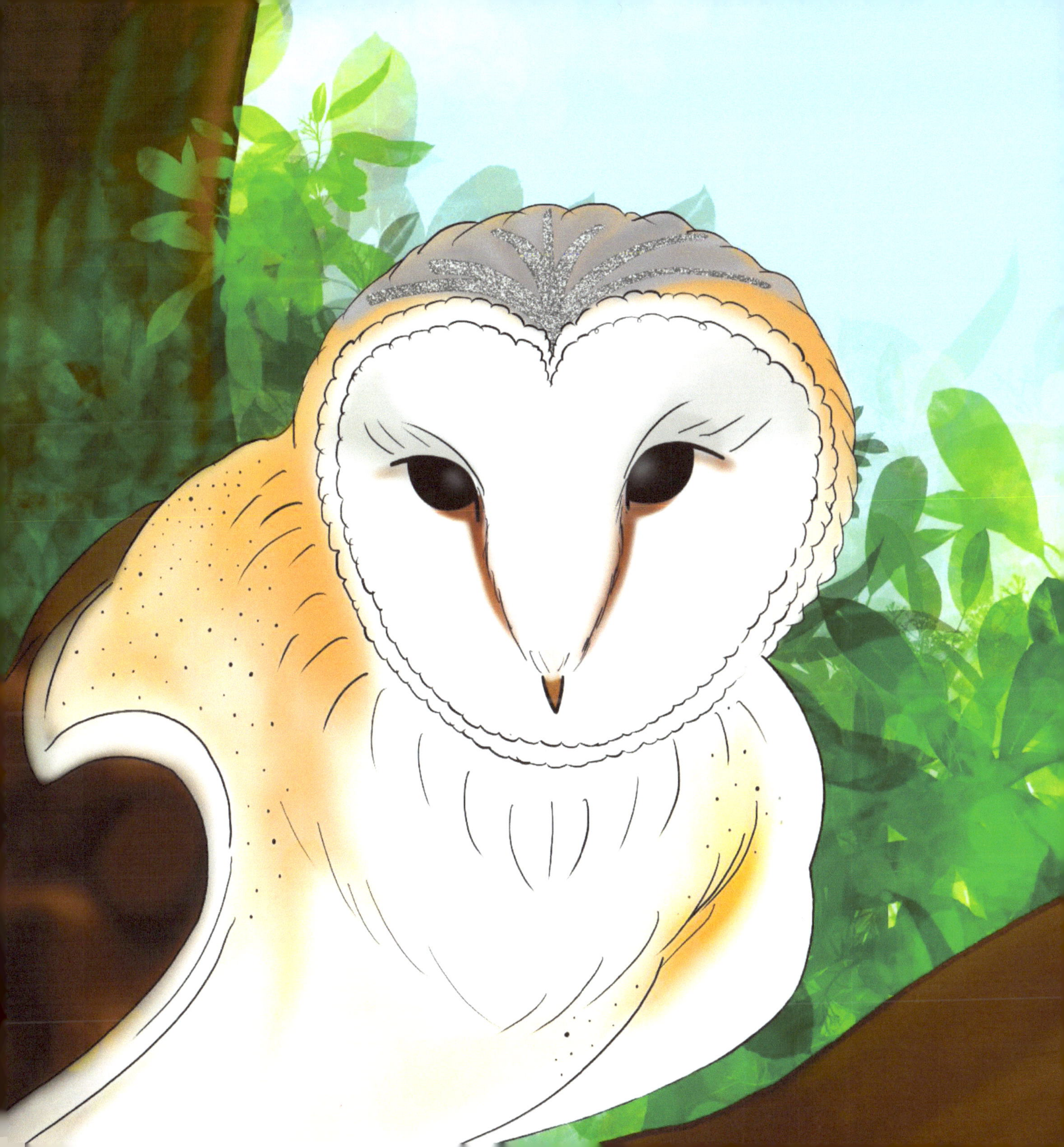

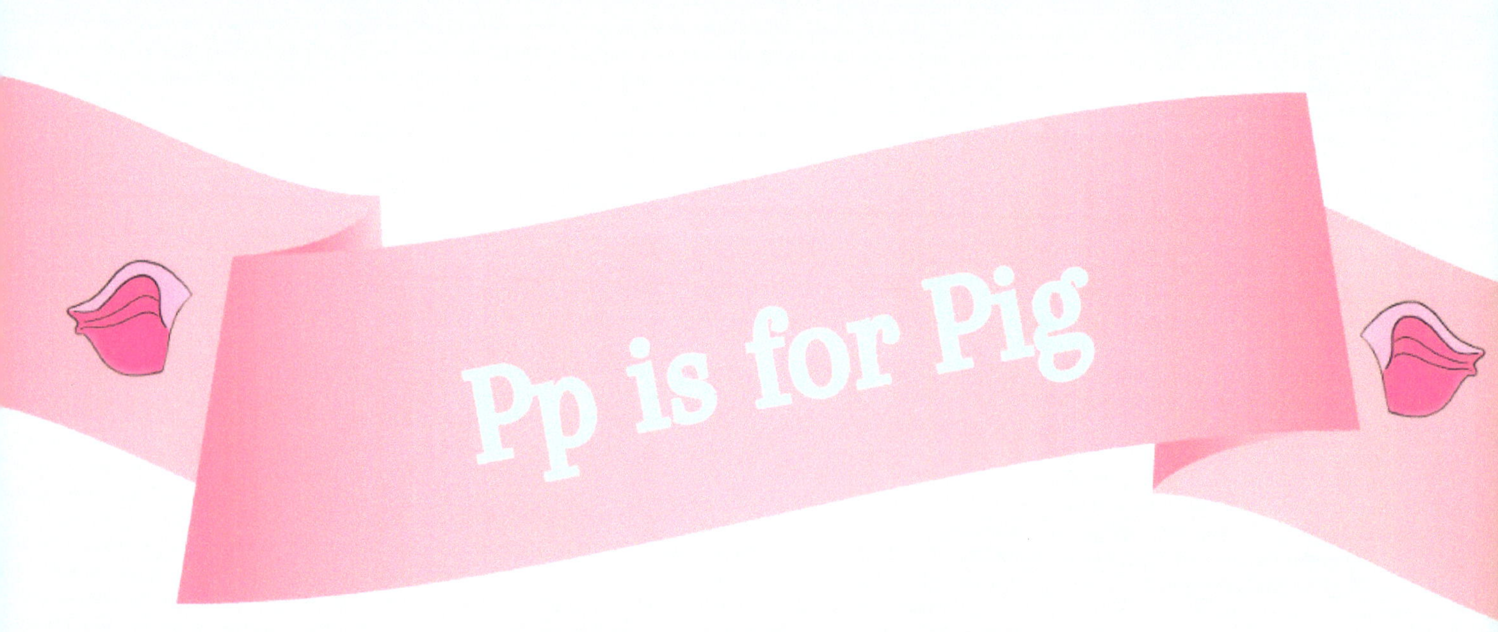

Rolling in the mud, happy as can be,
God made this animal snort with glee.

Have you ever seen a pig on a farm?

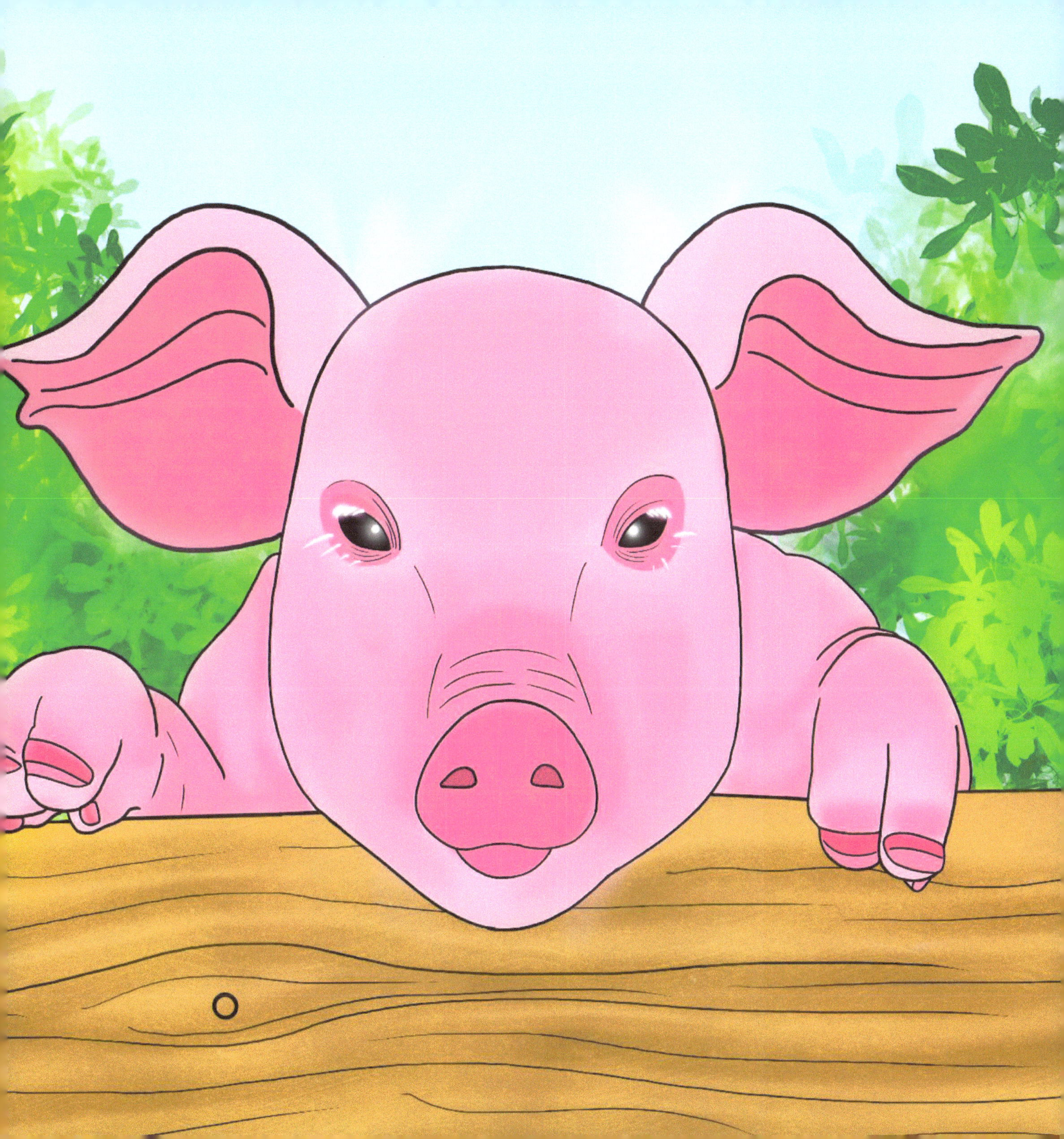

Qq is for Queen Alexandra Birdwing Butterfly

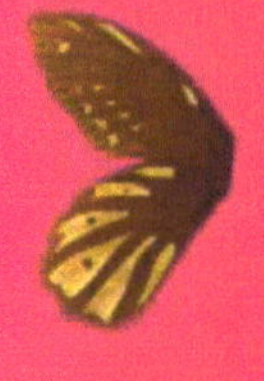

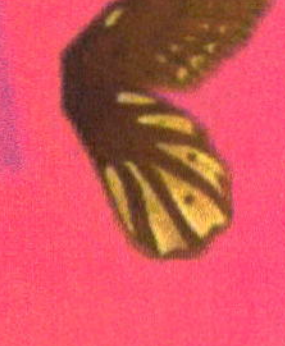

Colorful wings, a divine sight,
God made its patterns such a delight.

What colors would your wings be if you were a butterfly?

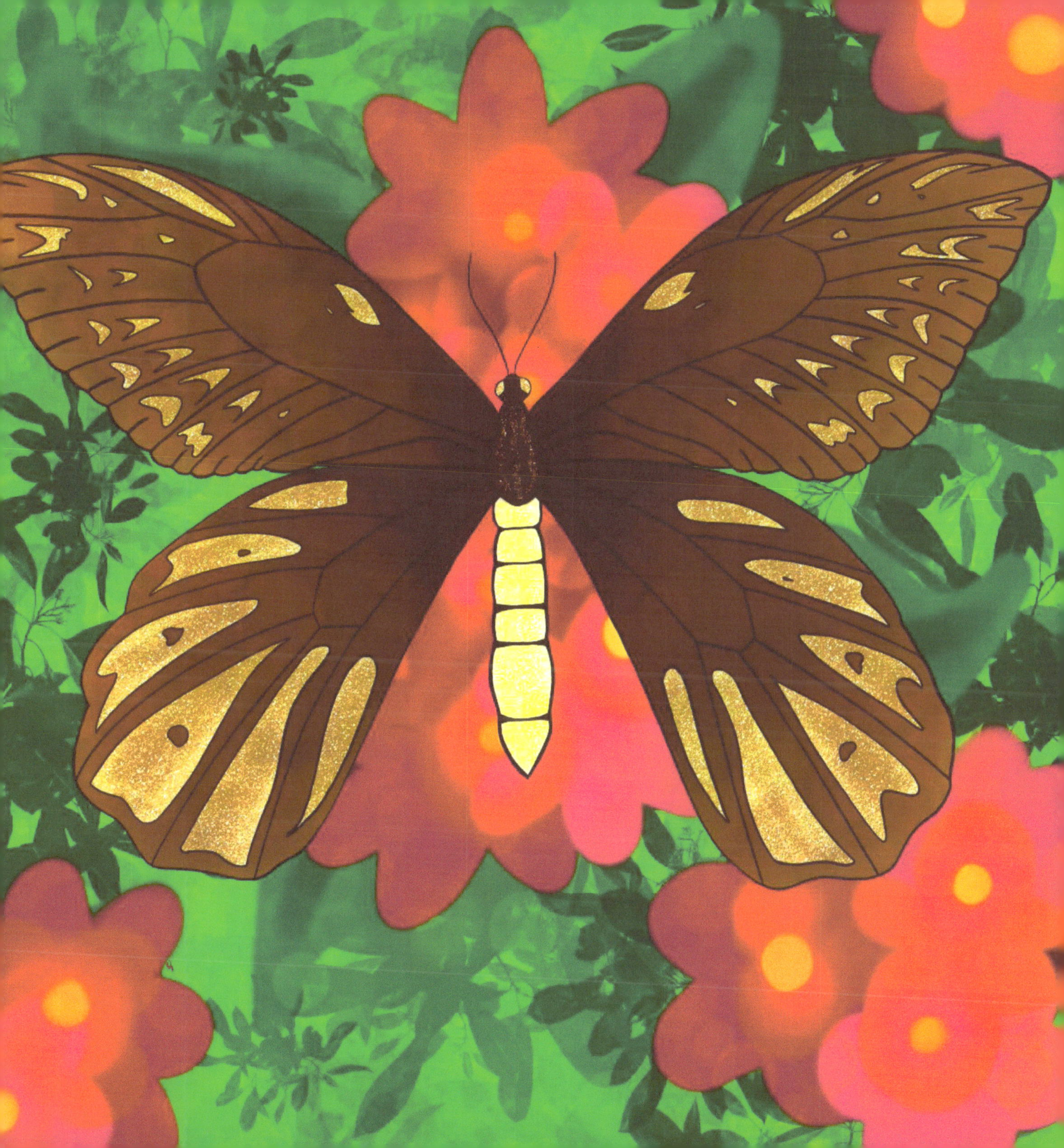

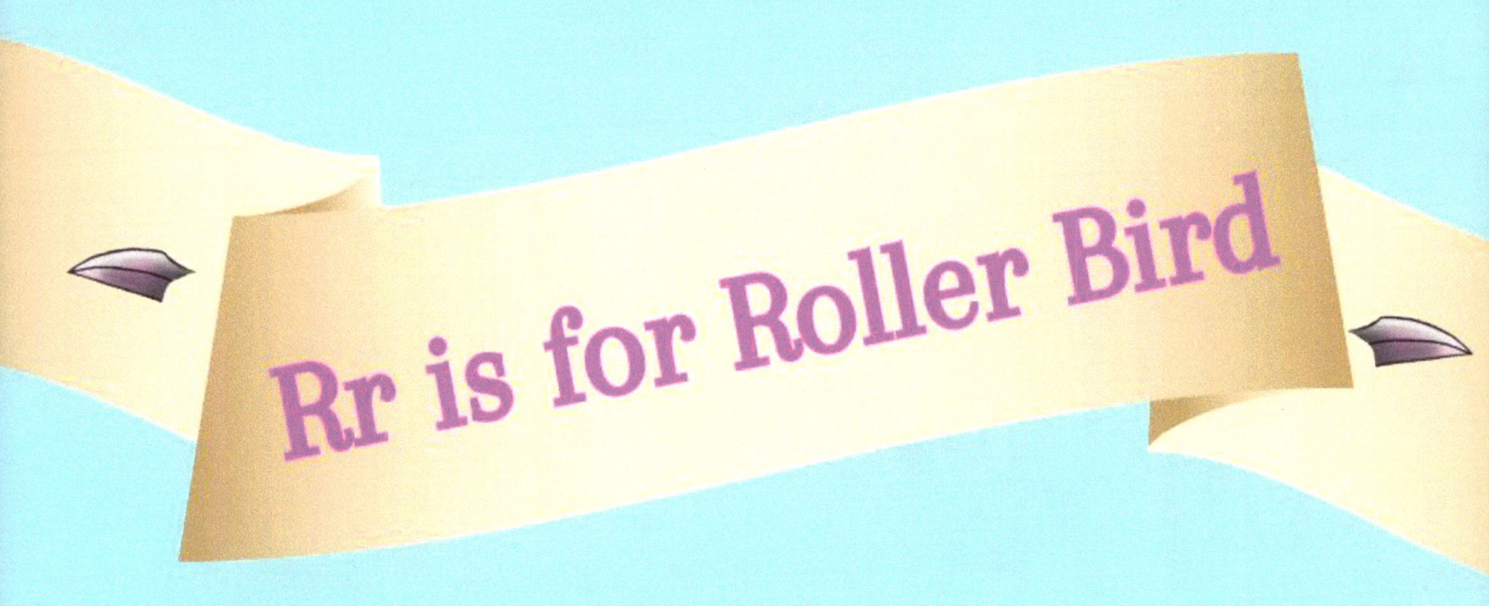

Flipping and flapping, dancing in the sky,
God made them twirl and whirl up high.

Can you dance like a Roller Bird?

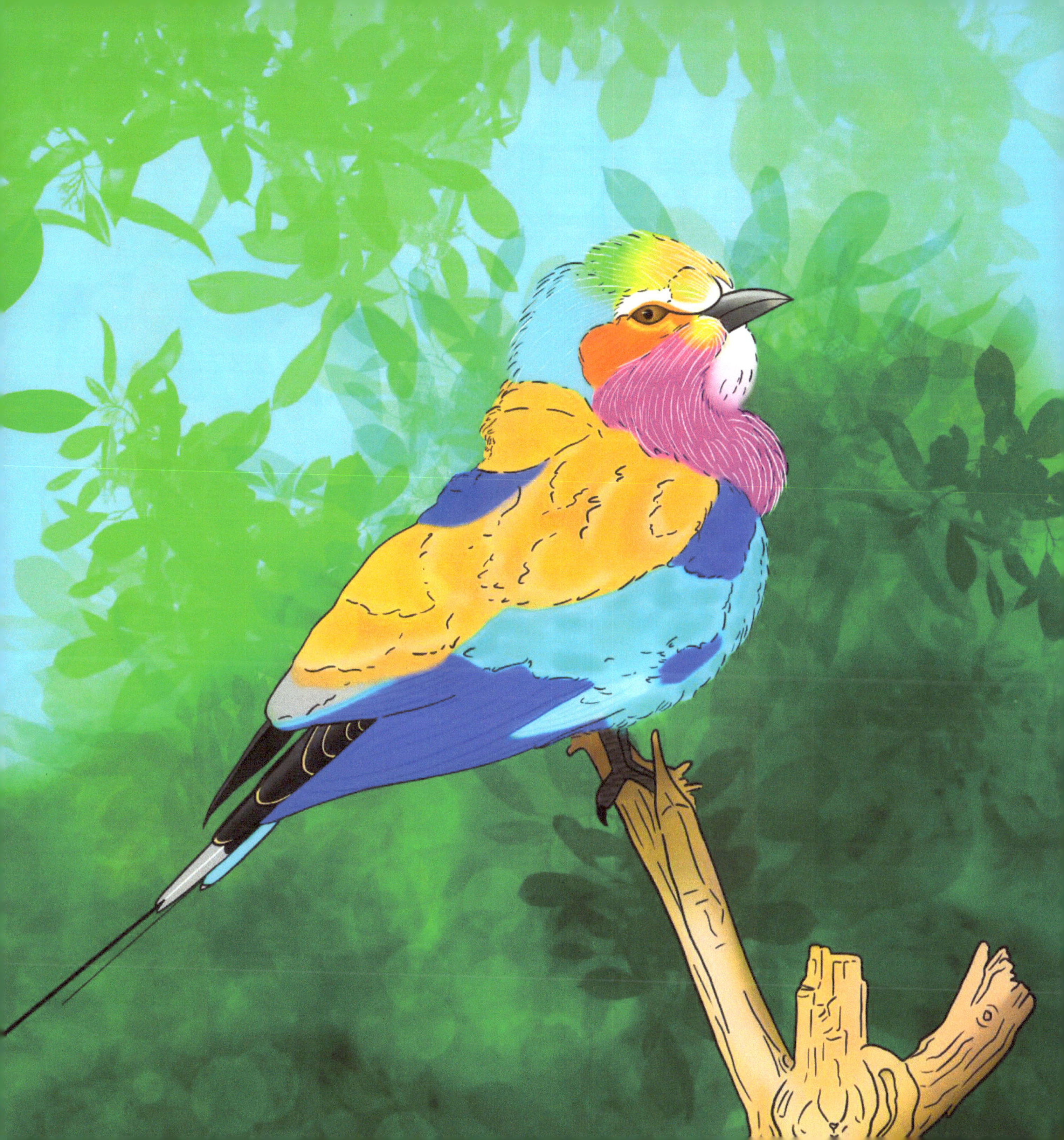

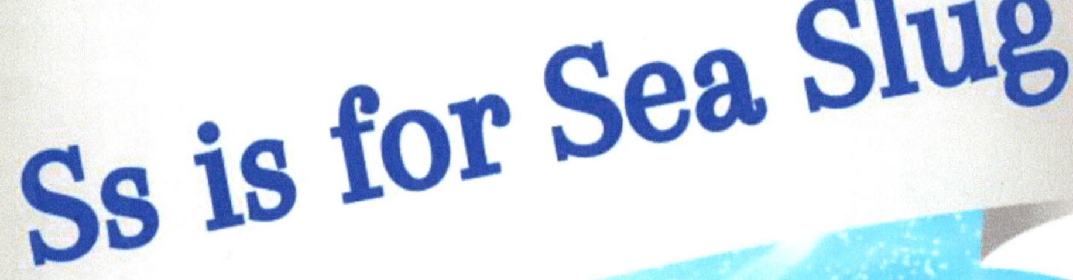

Colors galore, under the sea,
God made their colors a sight to see.

What is your favorite color sea slug?

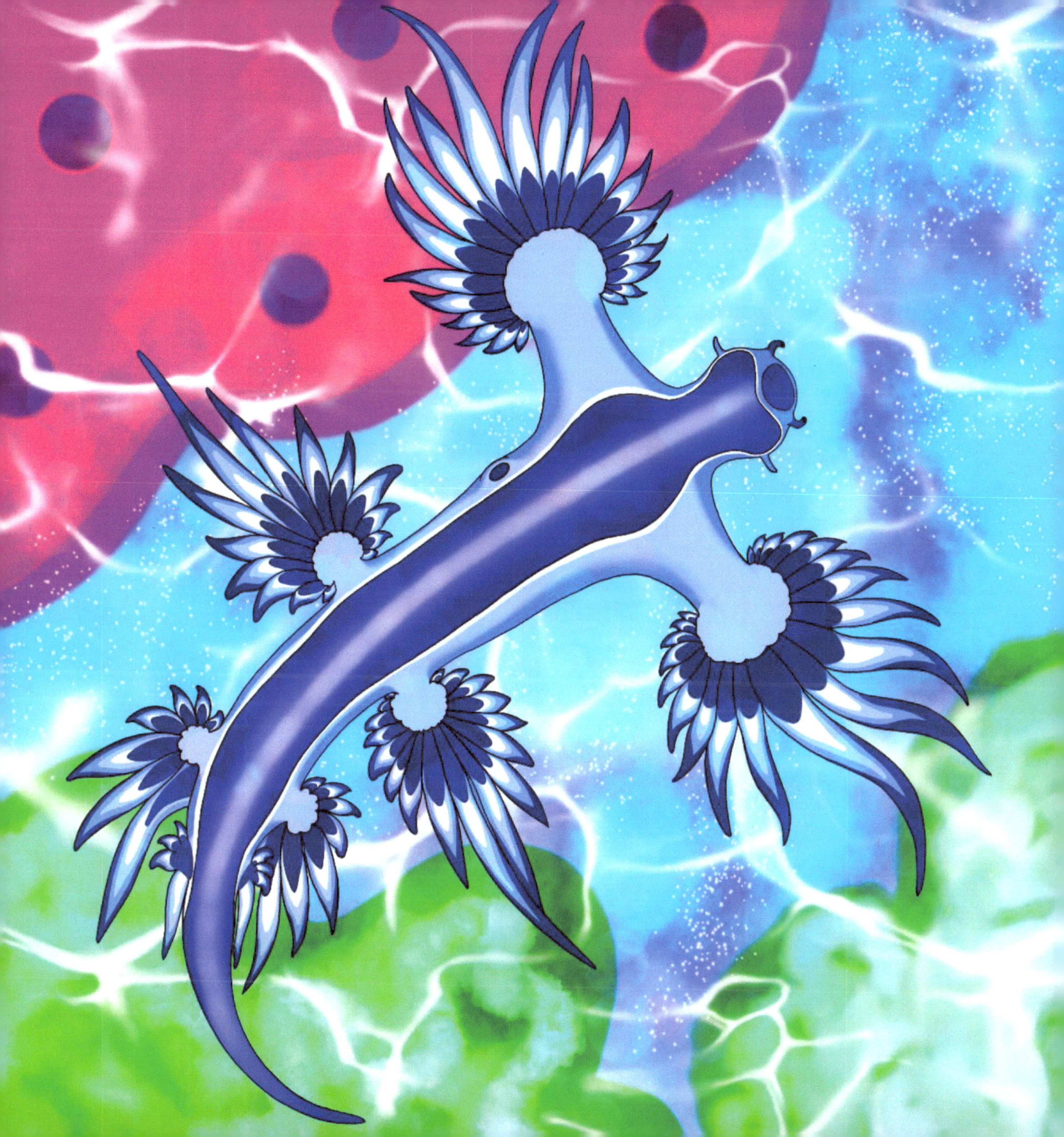

Tt is for Tiger

Colorful stripes, a stunning sight,
God made this cat bite with great might.

Can you pretend to be a tiger prowling in the jungle at night?

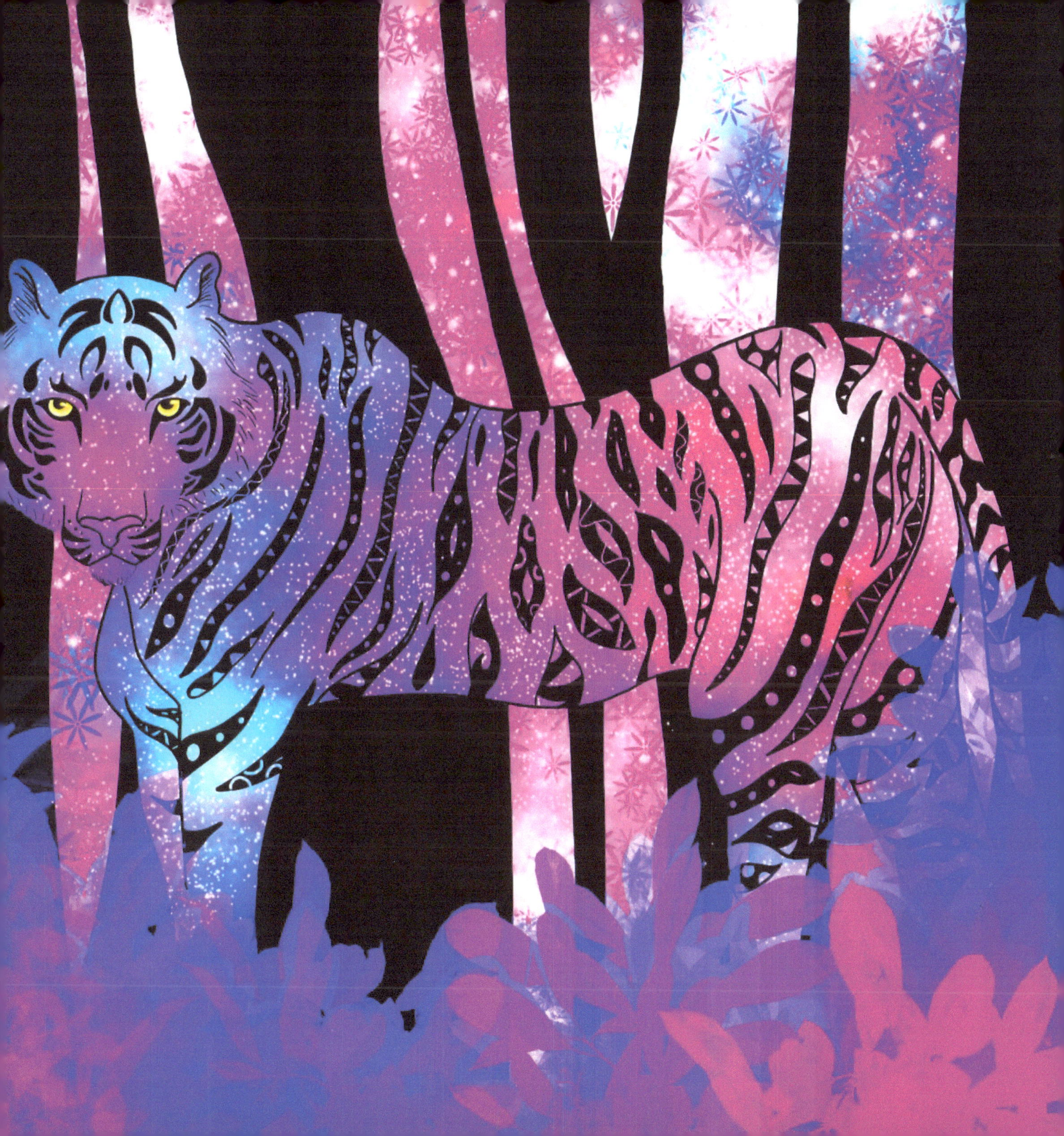

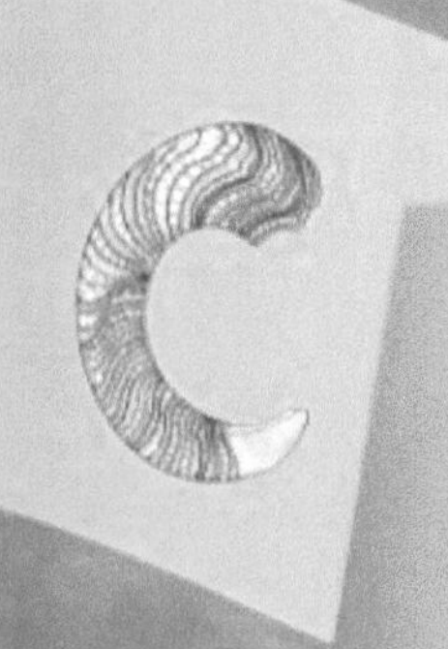

Uu is for Urial

Curvy horns, tough as rock,
God made this ram lead its flock.

Can you make finger horns like a Urial?

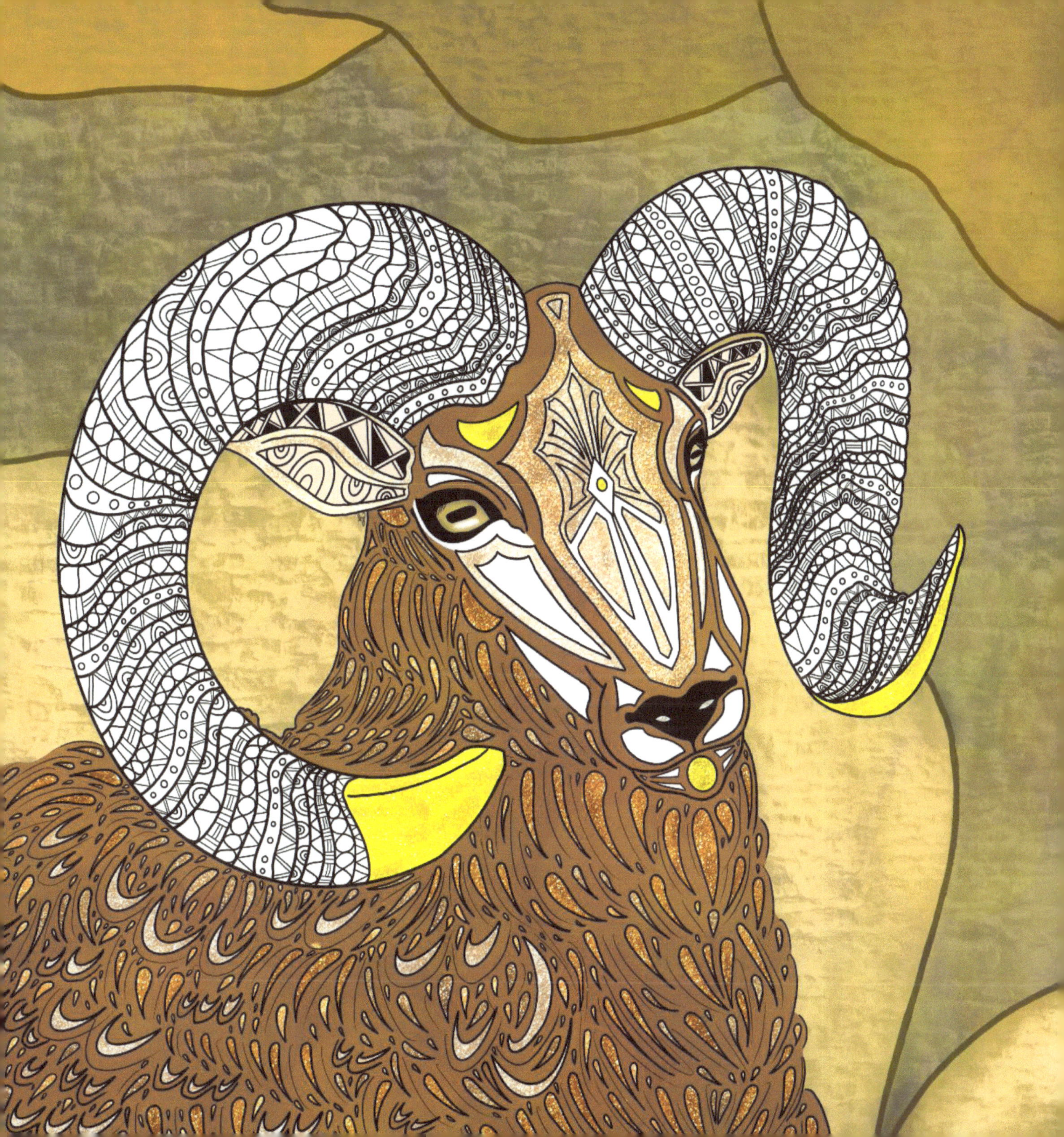

Vv is for Viper

Sidewinding reptile, so crafty and sly,
God made their tongues taste the sky.

Can you move silently like a viper?

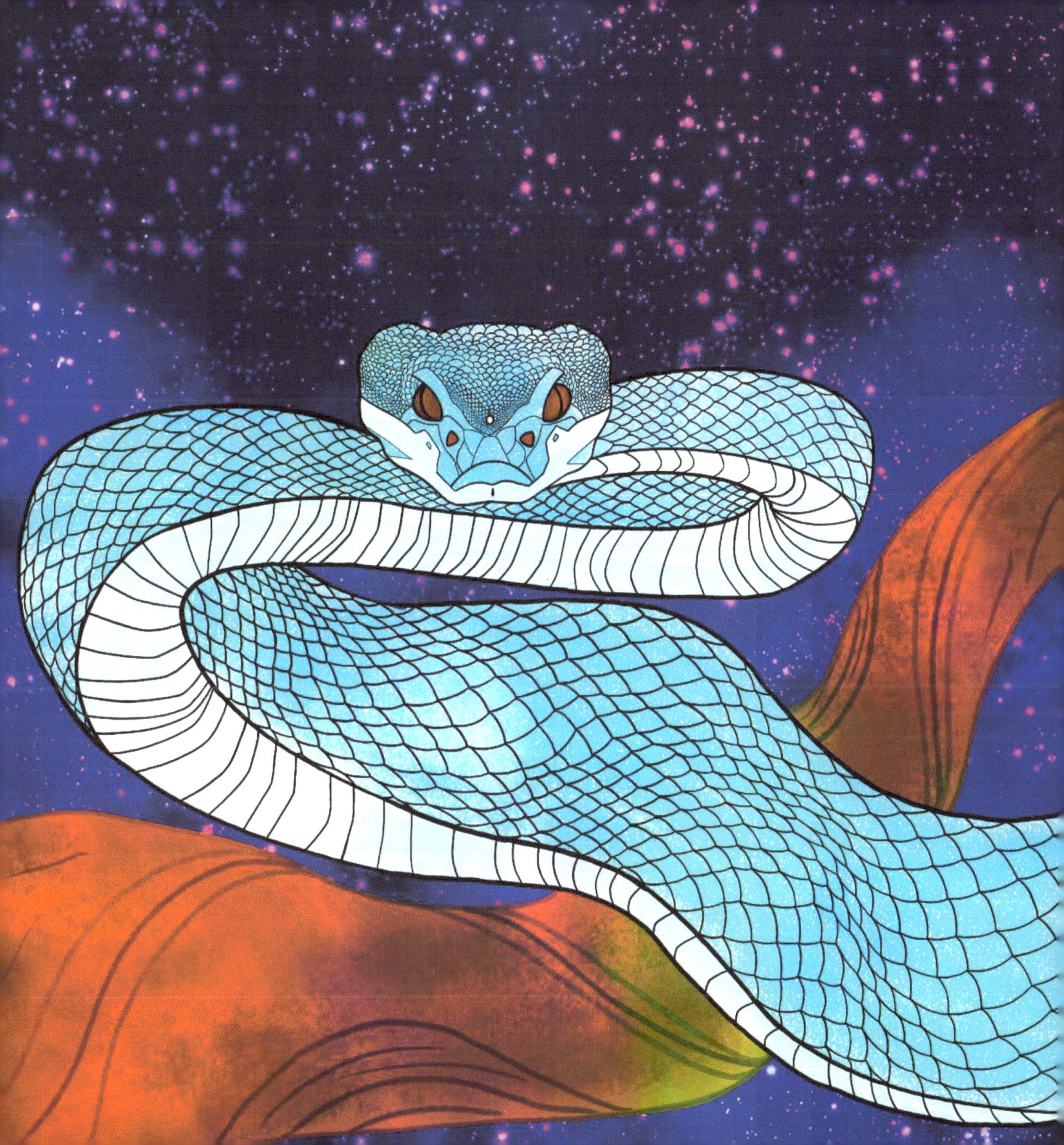

Ww is for Whale

In oceans deep, it hunts and dives,
God made them sleep with open eyes.

Have you ever seen a whale in the ocean?

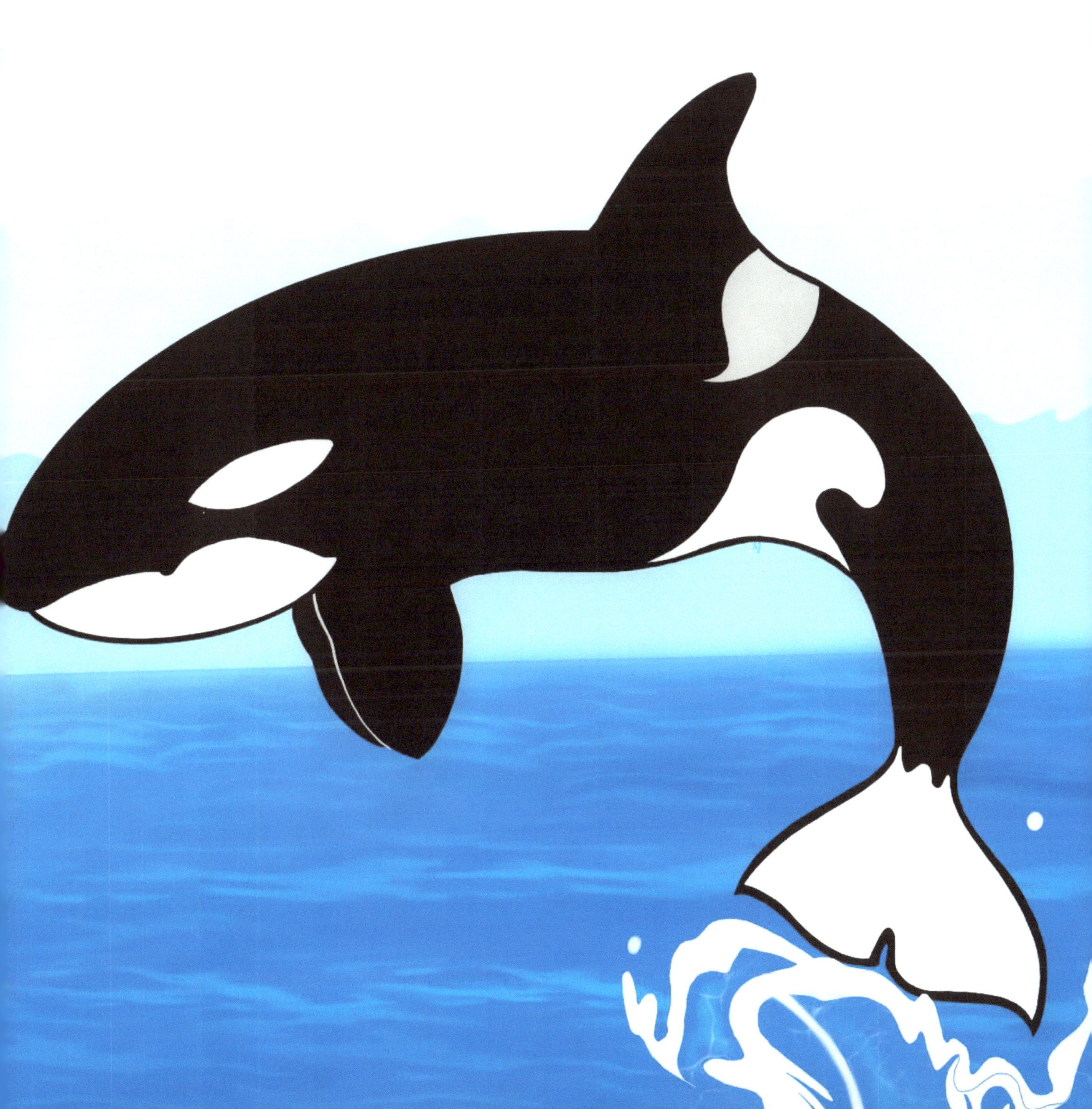

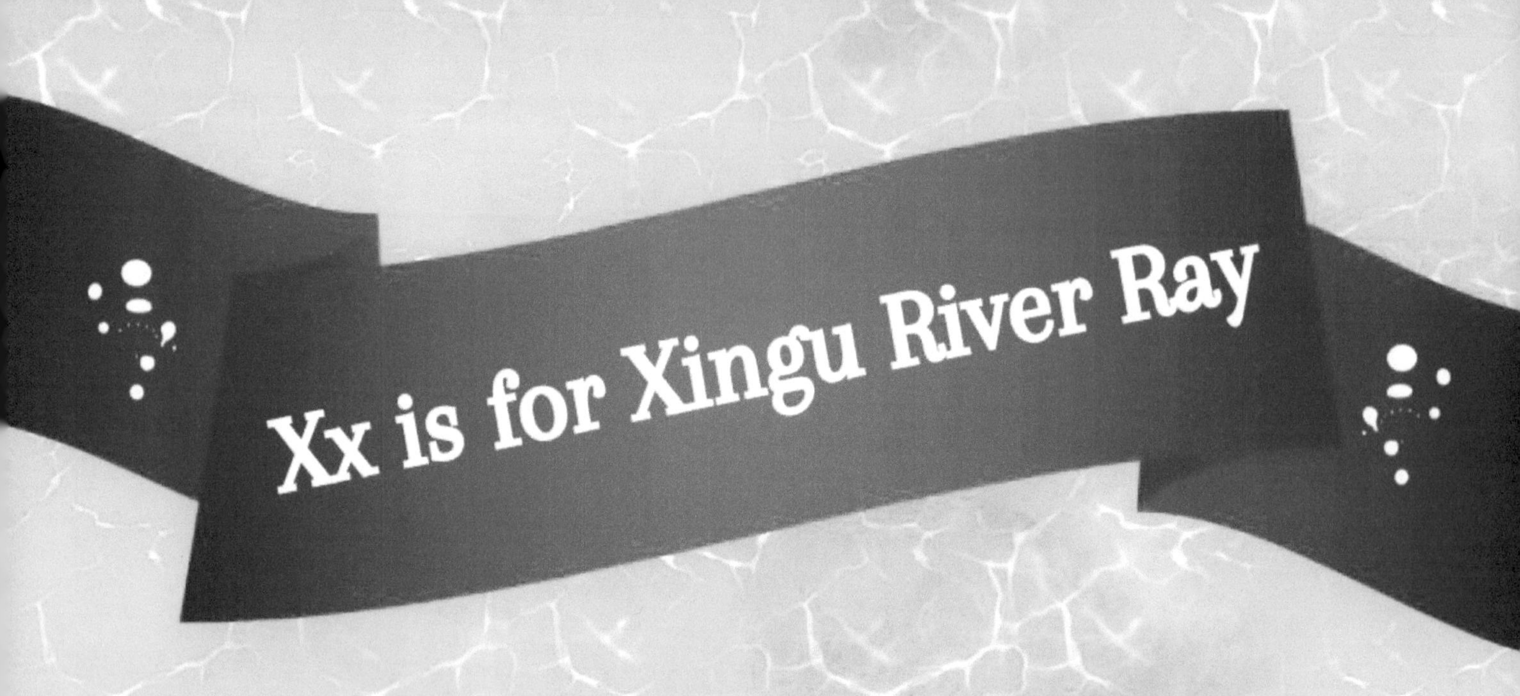

Xx is for Xingu River Ray

Spotted and speckled, lots of polka-dots,
God made this fish with venom and spots.

What pattern would you have if you were a stingray?

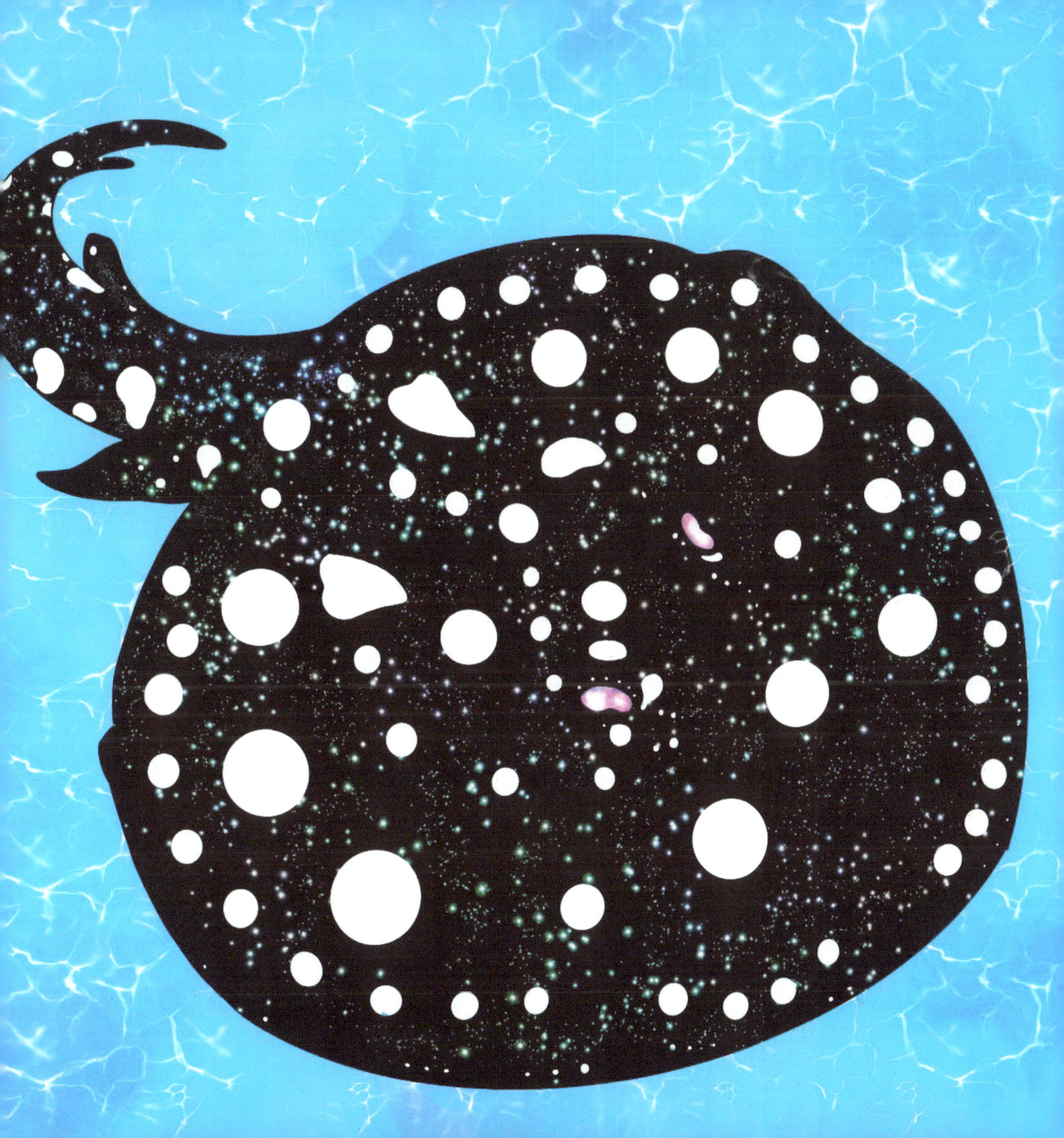

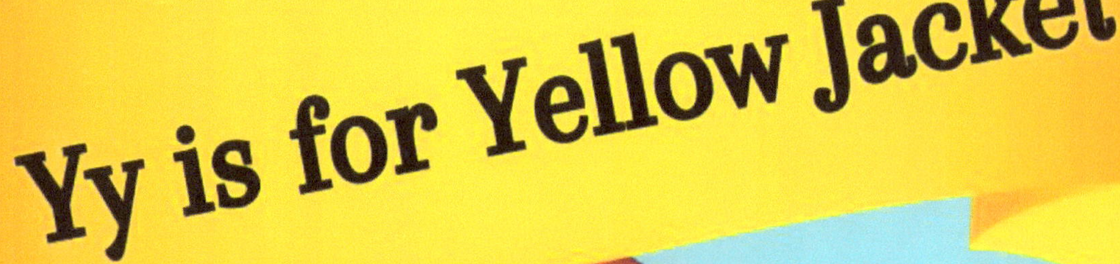

Yy is for Yellow Jacket

Buzzing around, yellow and black,
God made them sting back-to-back.

Can you buzz like a Yellow Jacket?

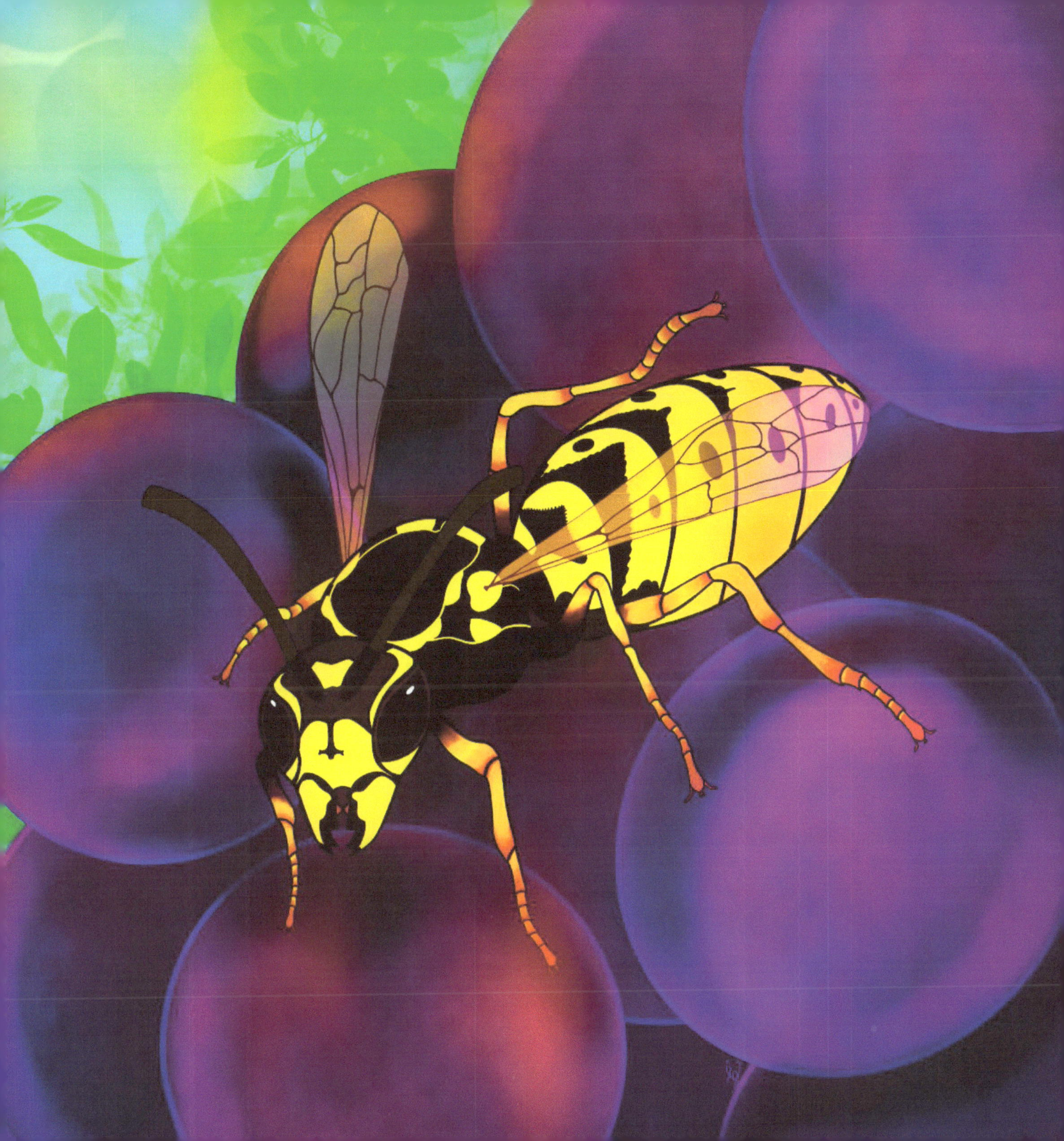

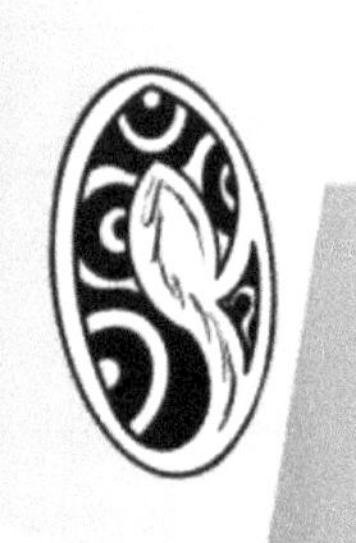

Zz is for Zebra

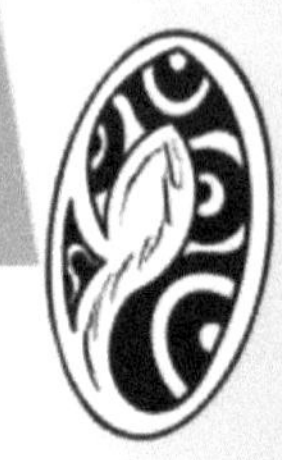

Stripes like fingerprints, each one has its own,
God made their patterns uniquely sewn.

What pattern would your stripes be if you were a zebra?

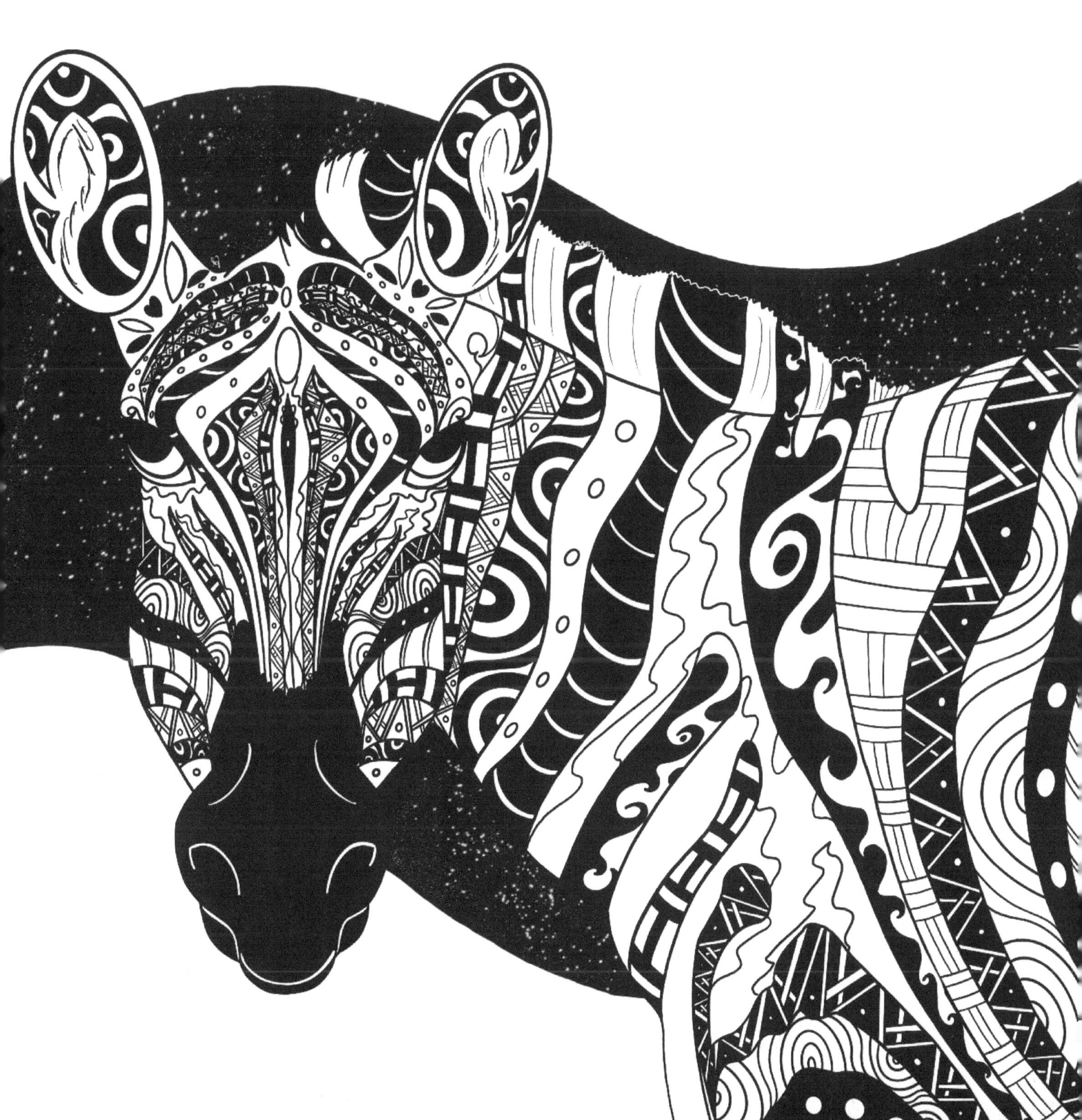

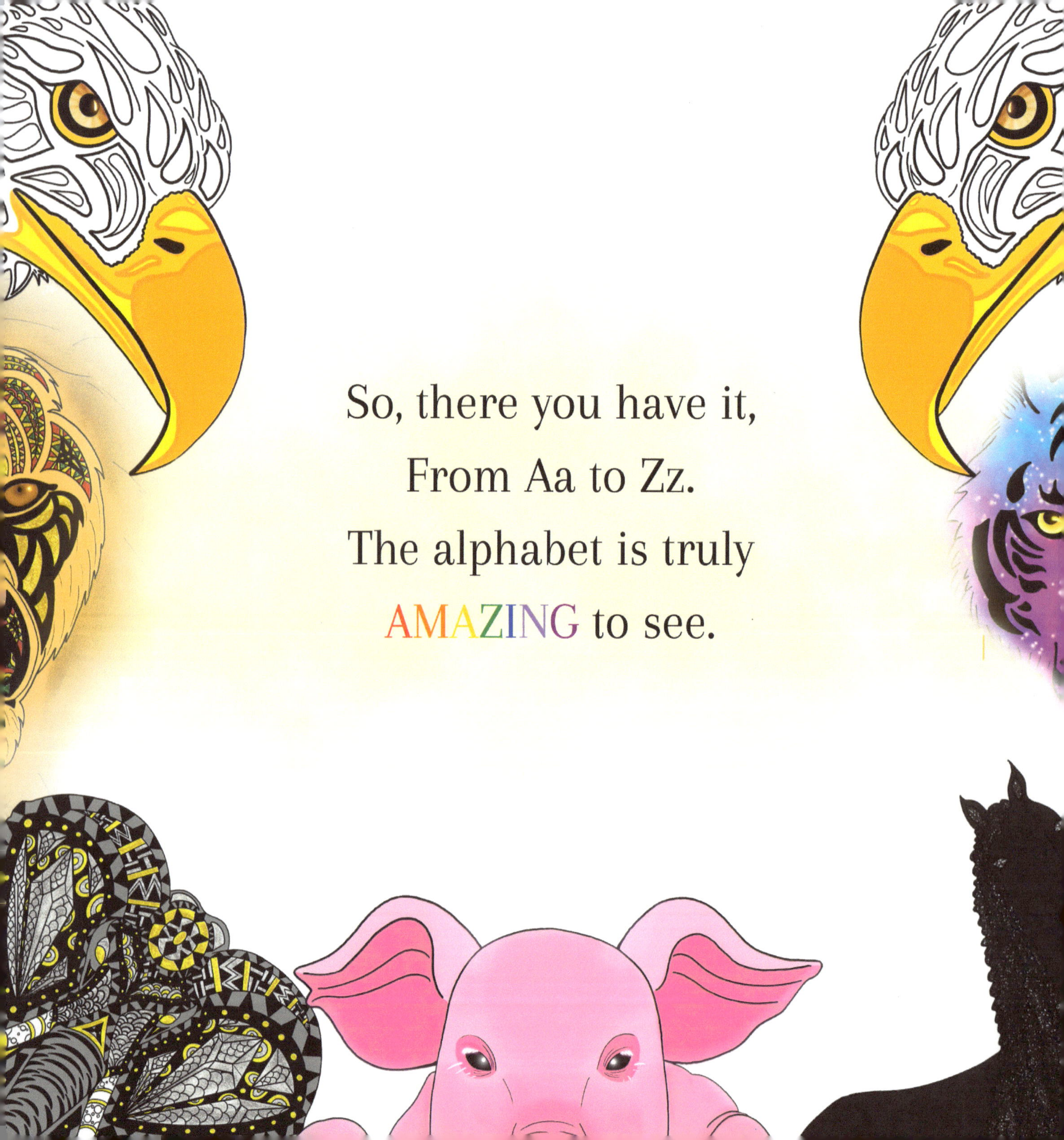

So, there you have it,
From Aa to Zz.
The alphabet is truly
AMAZING to see.

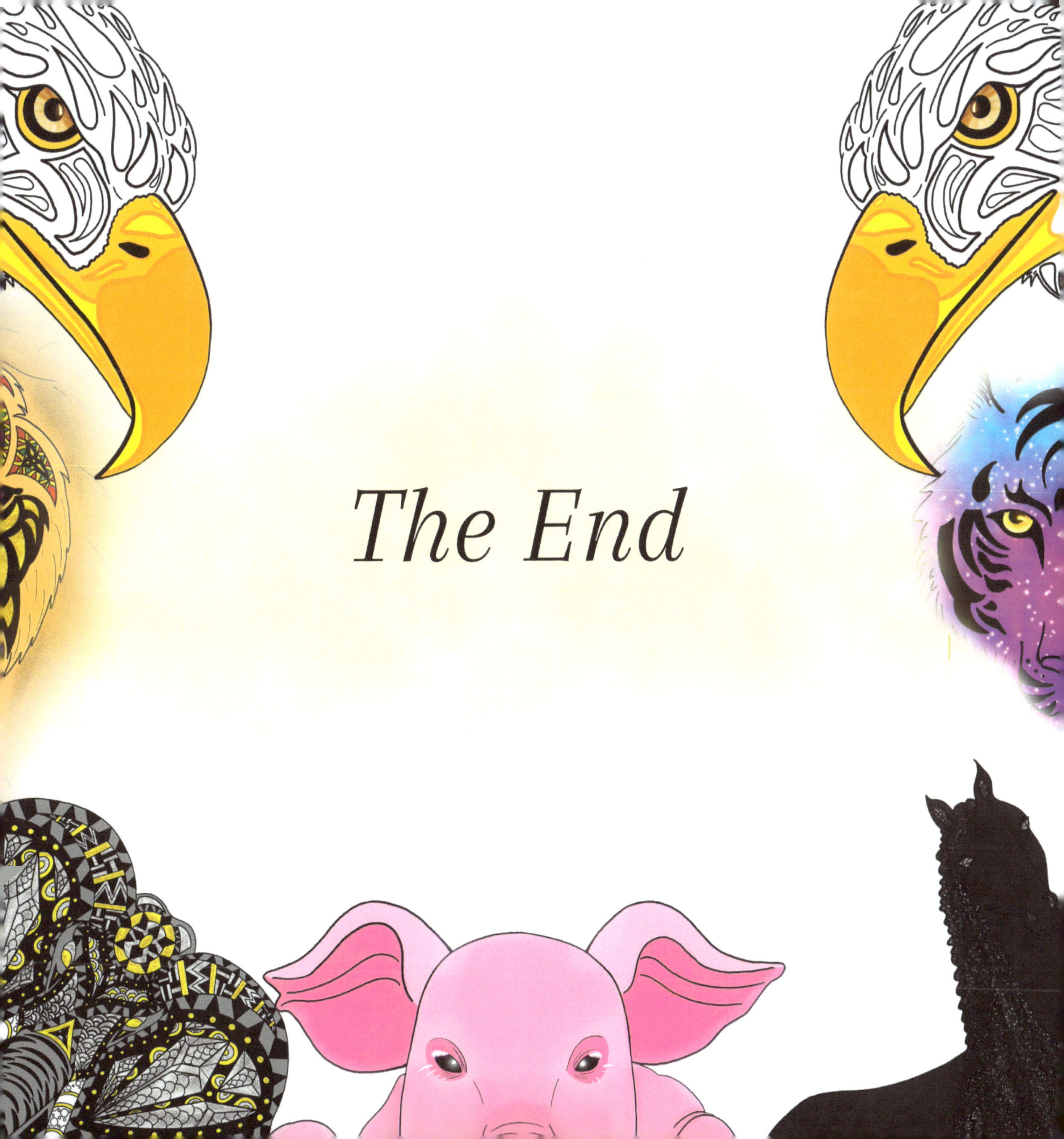

The End

MEET THE AUTHOR, ILLUSTRATOR, AND DESIGNER

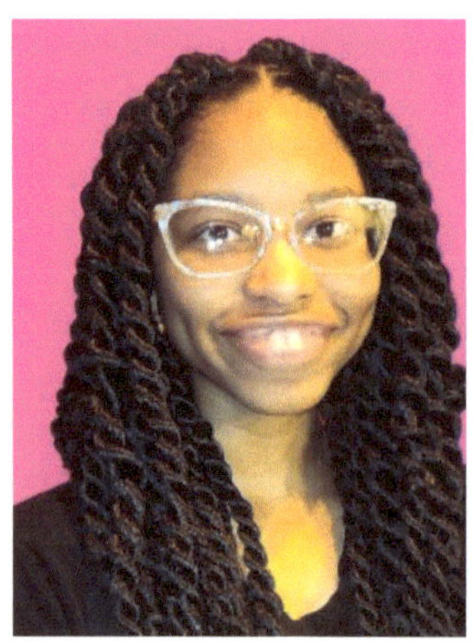

Meet Abigail C. Johnson, a vibrant 15-year-old author, illustrator, and keynote speaker, who is a shining star in the world of young writers. As a core member of the dynamic "JFAM JOHNSON™," Abigail has co-authored and illustrated three captivating books: "Hip Hop Hair," "The Flow Journal," and "Hip Hop Music." Her passion for storytelling and art leap off the pages, engaging readers of all ages. Her skills have been recognized by Book Authority, winning their "Best New Hip Hop Music Book" award.

Abigail isn't just about putting words on paper; she's a voice for youth empowerment in the literary world. Her insightful keynote speeches at the "R.I.S.E. Virtual Summit" in 2022 and 2023 have inspired many, sharing her journey as a young writer and offering invaluable advice to other teens and young adults eager to embark on their own publishing adventures.

What makes Abigail truly special is her commitment to a healthy, compassionate lifestyle as a vegetarian, and her incredible talent in drawing. These personal passions are reflected in her work, infusing her books with creativity, care, and a deep appreciation for life in all its forms.

For a dive into Abigail's imaginative world, her books are must-read. Each page resonates with her youthful energy and artistic flair. And there's more to explore! Visit www.abigailcjohnson.com to journey further into Abigail's world of creativity, inspiration, and literary brilliance. Join her as she continues to craft stories that captivate, illustrate worlds that dazzle, and inspire a new generation of young authors and artists.

AUTHOR'S INVITATION

Thank you for taking the time to read my book, and I hope you've enjoyed it! My book's purpose is to encourage, educate, and empower young people to be their very best. I would love to hear from you!

To support my efforts, or simply if you've enjoyed this book, please help me by:

1. **Giving my book a sincere review on Amazon or by posting on social media.** This will greatly help me share this book with others.

2. **Spreading the word.** You can let a close friend or family member borrow this book, or you can purchase additional copies to donate to your local school, homeless shelter, or church.

3. **Saying, "Hi!"** online and tagging us (@jfamjohnson and @umotiv8cre8tions), or by checking out our links page at https://beacons.ai/jfamjohnson.

4. **Signing up for our next Live event** to discover opportunities to write, draw, and publish your very own book. Just have your parent or guardian email my parents at admin@testimonypublishersllc.com using the subject line ***The Amazing Alphabet Live.***

5. **Inviting my family and me to be guests** at your next Live or virtual event. Whether your event is at your church, school, library, book fair, or on a podcast, or in a magazine, we'd love to make arrangements to speak, do a read-aloud, show you how to publish a book, or share our story.

Thanks in advance for your support!

OTHER BOOKS AND AWARDS BY THE AUTHOR

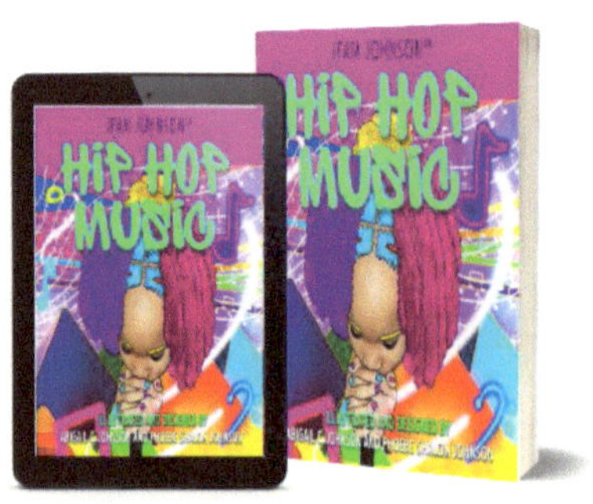

HIP HOP MUSIC

Bookauthority

BEST NEW HIP-HOP MUSIC BOOKS

WINNER

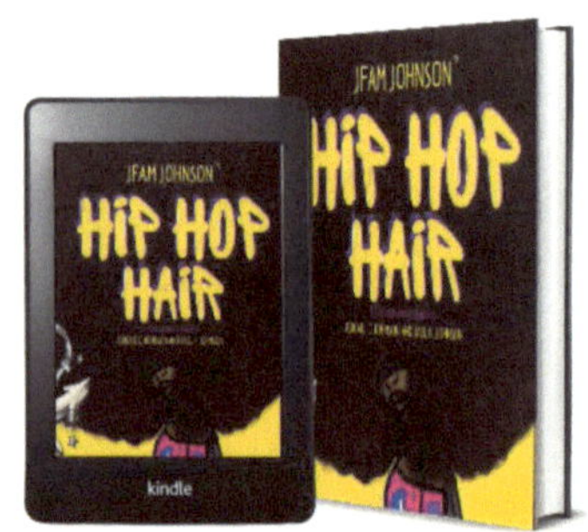

HIP HOP HAIR

Bookauthority

BEST NEW MUSIC BOOKS

WINNER

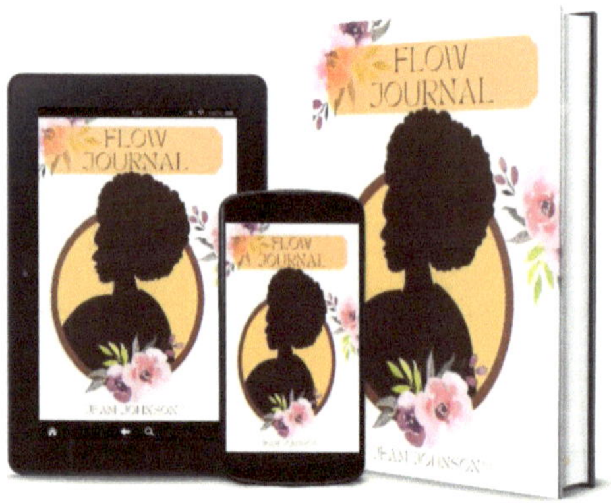

FLOW JOURNAL

www.ingramcontent.com/pod-product-compliance
Lightning Source LLC
LaVergne TN
LVHW070149110826
845147LV00002B/354

* 9 7 8 1 7 3 6 0 1 8 7 8 1 *